The Song of Songs

שיר השירים
אשר לשלמה

The Song of Songs

A New Translation and Interpretation

MARCIA FALK

Illustrated by Barry Moser

HarperSanFrancisco
A Division of HarperCollins*Publishers*

Frontispiece
Illustration:

כְּשׁוֹשַׁנָּה בֵּין הַחוֹחִים
כֵּן רַעְיָתִי בֵּין הַבָּנוֹת

᠌᠌᠊᠊᠊

Narcissus in the brambles,
Brightest flower—

THE SONG OF SONGS: *A New Translation and Interpretation.*
Copyright © 1973, 1977, 1982, 1990 by Marcia Lee Falk.
Illustrations copyright © 1990 by Pennyroyal Press, Inc. All rights
reserved. Printed in the United States of America. No part of this
book may be used or reproduced in any manner whatsoever
without written permission except in the case of brief quotations
embodied in critical articles and reviews. For information address
HarperCollins Publishers, 10 East 53rd Street, New York, NY
10022.

FIRST HarperCollins edition published in 1990.

Library of Congress Cataloging-in-Publication Data
Bible. O. T. Song of Solomon. English. Falk. 1990.
  The Song of songs / Marcia Falk.
    p.   cm.
  Rev. ed. of: Love lyrics from the Bible. 1982.
  ISBN 0-06-062339-X
    1. Bible. O. T. Song of Solomon—Translating. 2. Bible.
  O. T. Song of Solomon—Criticism, interpretation, etc.
  I. Falk, Marcia.   II. Falk, Marcia. Love lyrics from the Bible.
  III. Title.
  BS1483.F35   1990   90-80329
  223'.905209—dc20   CIP

90 91 92 93 94 RRD(H) 10 9 8 7 6 5 4 3 2 1

This edition is printed on acid-free paper that meets the
American National Standards Institute Z39.48 Standard.

For Abraham Gilead—
my future and my joy

Contents

Author's Note:
History and Acknowledgments

THE JOURNEY OF TRANSLATION always begins with the text. Yet sometimes there is an earlier journey—the story of how the translator came to the text. This book had its origin in the early 1970s, when I was a doctoral student in English and comparative literature at Stanford and found myself dissatisfied with the limits of the traditional academic curriculum. My growing need at that time, as a woman and a Jew, for sources more directly connected to my own origins led me in search of Hebrew literature that included the authentic voices of women. Although I had studied the Hebrew Bible from childhood on, I wasn't sure it had what I was now looking for. But then a memory rose up of a part of the Bible that had engaged me the first time I heard it chanted, in my adolescence. I didn't know much about it; yet, especially as a poet, I felt somehow called to it—if for no other reason than its haunting musicality. As I began to study, I soon saw what a remarkable book this was, one in which the voices of women and men were heard celebrating eros, sensuality, and the pleasures of nature. I was first enchanted, then soon engrossed in this small, unique Hebrew text: the Song of Songs.

Coincidentally, at the time I began my study of the Song I was enrolled in a poets' workshop on verse translation. One night the workshop members met for a party, and as I talked about my new discovery I quickly realized that my classmates were unfamiliar with the text I was speaking of. Indeed, the Song of Songs that they knew from the standard English versions of the Bible was quite different from the one that had me in its thrall. That night someone suggested that I try my hand at my own translation. I went home and began.

By the mid-seventies, my renditions of individual poems from the Song of Songs were circulating in literary magazines, and in 1977 the full collection first appeared in print. In 1982 a scholarly edition containing the translation and an initial version of the translator's study was published in Great Britain. The edition that you now hold in your hands offers to both general readers and scholars the complete translation and an updated version of the study, along with, for the first time, the vocalized Hebrew text of the Masoretic (standard) Hebrew Bible, presented as I have reconstructed it in a sequence of lyric poems. Readers who want to use my reconstruction of the Hebrew text orally will, I hope, find here an easily readable form.

While my overall view of the Song of Songs as a lyric anthology has not changed since I first formulated my ideas about it, new readings of specific passages have occurred to me over the past decade and are incorporated in this edition. Some of these reflect consideration of recent scholarship, specifically literary study of the Bible; in addition, the work of feminist scholars, both within and beyond the area of Bible study, has stimulated my thinking. Much has changed in the study of literature since the early 1970s, when my modest proposal of a literary critique of the Bible that included feminist insights was received by some as shocking. (I recall one professor who cautioned me, early on, to separate myself as a feminist from myself as a translator. I replied that I was grateful not to have to do any such violence to myself, since the Song of Songs was not the sexist text that he apparently took it to be.) I am gratified to find that my instincts of two decades ago, in regard to the selection and interpretation of this book, have led me in directions that still feel right, and fruitful, today. And it is a relief to find that paths I once embarked on more or less alone are now more commonly and comfortably traveled.

When I first began my research on the Song of Songs in 1971, literary analysis of the Bible was relatively untilled terrain; I had to combine the resources of two university departments, English and Religious Studies, to evolve my approach to interpretation and translation. Many people, including Bible scholars, literary critics, and poets, supported my efforts during that period, and to all of them I remain grateful. To one, however, I must reiterate my appreciation: *Author's Note* Edwin Good, of the Stanford Religious Studies Department, was the first Bible scholar with whom I studied the Song of Songs and the person who inspired my path as I sought ways to combine Bible scholarship with literary criticism.

A number of Israeli experts also offered crucial assistance while I was conducting my research. I thank Nogah Hareuveni and his staff at Neot Kedumim (the Gardens of Israel) for their help in identifying flora and fauna in the Hebrew text. I am grateful to Chaim Rabin, of the Hebrew Language Department at the Hebrew University, for answering my queries about obscure words in the original text, and to Moshe Greenberg, of the Bible Department at the Hebrew University, for debating with me my interpretations of the Hebrew text and for encouraging me to persevere at my renditions.

For various kinds of editorial, bibliographic, and technical assistance at later stages of the book, I am indebted to Lillian Steinfeld, Anne Geissman Canright, Carleen Carman, David Langenberg, Hillel Furstenberg, Ari Davidow, and Jack Love. For keeping my telephones working, thank you, Sam. To Kandace Hawkinson goes my appreciation for facilitating the publication of the book with competence and grace.

I wish also to acknowledge the Stanford English Department, which provided support and fellowship assistance for several years; the Fulbright-Hays Foundation, which gave me a grant in Bible and Hebrew literature in 1973–74; and the Hebrew University of Jerusalem, which awarded me a postdoctoral fellowship in Hebrew language and literature to continue my research in 1978–79.

I have been sustained in a different way by the support of several communities—especially the Jewish renewal and *havurah* movements—which have kept my version of the Song of Songs alive for years, beginning before it was formally published and including long periods when it was hard to find or out of print. I was encouraged by hearing my translation read dramatically on radio and stage, set to music and

Author's Note sung, recited at wedding ceremonies, and chanted on the Sabbath of Passover. To all those who embraced my work and made it part of a new oral tradition, I am enormously grateful: you nourished the poet's soul, perhaps more than you know.

Finally, warmest appreciation goes to Steve Rood, my best and most faithful reader, for his tireless review of draft upon draft of this work. To my first teachers—Abraham Abbey Falk, of blessed memory, and Frieda Goldberg Falk— goes my immeasurable gratitude for pointing the way.

Berkeley, California
1990

Preface

ONE OF THE MOST CELEBRATED collections of ancient love poetry, the Song of Songs—also known in English as the Song of Solomon, and referred to, by scholars, simply as the Song—is the only book of love poetry in the Bible and as such has been the subject of much speculation and controversy. For centuries, both Jewish and Christian traditions viewed the Song as spiritual allegory, thus justifying its place in the biblical canon; but this mode of interpretation, moving and imaginative as it may be, does not explain the text's primary level of meaning. Another centuries-old interpretation presents the Song as a drama with fixed characters, such as King Solomon and a country bride or King Solomon and two country lovers. But it is difficult to find evidence of dramatic structure in the Song; acts, scenarios, and characters are not indicated, and there is hardly a trace of coherent plot. Rather, the Song has a variety of contexts that shift frequently in no apparent dramatic sequence and within which many different kinds of voices speak. There is no reason to assume only a few fixed speakers in the Song, and even less justification for viewing Solomon as a central character. Although Solomon's name is mentioned in the Hebrew title, this title was bestowed not by the Song's original author or authors but by later compilers, who were likely also responsible for giving the text its semblance of structural unity. In its earliest stages, the Song was probably not a unified work at all, but several lyric poems, each having its own integrity.

About the Song's authorship and origins very little is known. Tradition ascribes the work to King Solomon, but this view is discounted by modern scholars, who generally agree that the Song's authorship cannot be specified. Indeed, there is no consensus even about the date of composition, with proposals ranging from 950 to 200 B.C.E.; some hold that the Song was composed by several authors over an ex-

Preface   tended period of time and compiled between 500 and 200 B.C.E.

In the past two centuries, scholars have hypothesized about the original context and function of the Song, proposing, for example, that it was a cycle of wedding songs or the liturgy of an ancient fertility cult. These theories, however, are not only unprovable but unconvincing, because they attempt to force the varied material in the text into single, confining molds. It is finally simpler and more illuminating to view the Song as a variegated collection of different types of lyric love poems that did not all necessarily derive from a single author or serve the same function in their original society. The stylistic similarities and repetitions among the poems are best explained as literary conventions of ancient Hebrew verse, particularly if one accepts the view that the Song was, in its earliest stages, popular oral literature. I believe it likely that the Song was orally composed and transmitted over an extended period before being transcribed, compiled, and finally canonized.

The reconstruction of the Hebrew text presented in this volume is based on this view of the Song; the particular division into thirty-one poems is my own, the result of literary analysis. Although many scholars today view the Song as a collection, the particular decisions concerning where one poem ends and the next begins are not obvious, and no two analyses are exactly alike. The Masoretic text (the standardized Hebrew text, edited by early medieval scholars known as Masoretes), as we have it in the Leningrad MS. (one of the oldest complete manuscripts of the Hebrew Bible, heavily relied on in contemporary scholarship), is divided into portions for synagogue reading, which may have been considered poetic units. But these divisions can hardly be regarded as definitive delineations of the original, orally transmitted poems. Any reconstruction is therefore a *postulation* of the boundaries of the original poems. Using the text of the Leningrad MS., with no alteration of sequence, I divided the Song into poems as I perceived them, basing my decisions on such considerations as changes in speakers, audiences, settings, tones of voice, moods, and arguments. I

made no emendations or changes to the words or cantillation marks of the text itself. I then translated the Hebrew
poems individually, giving each its own form in English.
Thus the English poems are divided into stanzas and lines
according to the demands of English poetic craft, and these
prosodic divisions do not necessarily correspond to those in
the Hebrew. I translated the entire Song of Songs with the
exception of chapter 6, verse 12—a line that has plagued commentators for centuries and for which I could arrive at no
satisfactory interpretation. Following this preface is a key indicating the biblical chapters and verses to which each poem
corresponds.

The typefaces used in the printing of the English poems
require some explanation. Three different kinds of voices
speak in the Song: singular female, singular male, and a
group of speakers. In the original, these are usually distin-
guishable because in Hebrew, various parts of speech, including the pronoun "you," have gender and number. So, for
example, if a speaker says "I love you" in Hebrew, we know
whether a man or a woman is being addressed; by assuming
a heterosexual relationship (a valid assumption for the
Song), we can also deduce the gender of the speaker. Without such grammatical clues, it would often be difficult to
know who is speaking in the Song, particularly because the
voices do not conform to masculine and feminine stereo-
types. Because English does not convey gender grammati-
cally as Hebrew does, the English poems are printed in three
typefaces. Throughout the translation, passages spoken by a
female voice are in roman (as in poem 1), passages spoken by
a male voice are in *italic* (as in poem 4), and passages spoken
by an unidentifiable voice or by a group of voices are in
SMALL CAPITALS (as in poem 11).

Because many of the poems are dialogues and a few are
spoken by three different voices, different typefaces appear
within individual poems. In any given poem, each typeface
represents a consistent speaker; however, the typefaces do
not necessarily imply consistent speakers from poem to
poem. Thus, for example, the female speaker of the first
stanza of poem 7 is the same as the speaker of that poem's

Preface third stanza, but not necessarily the same as the female speaker of poem 8.

ಶಾ

But why this new translation of the Song, a book that has been translated, interpreted, arranged, and—to use Franz Rosenzweig's image—"convulsed" many times? By far the most acclaimed English version is that found in the King James Bible, which, although it treats the Song no differently from biblical prose, achieves a level of grace and eloquence that earns it a unique place among English classics. Still, from the perspective of scholarship, the King James Version is long outdated. Our understanding of the Hebrew text has changed considerably since the time of King James, and one of the offshoots of modern research has been a series of new Bible translations. Some of the new English Bibles that have been completed in the last few decades are the Revised Standard Version (1952), *The Jerusalem Bible* (1966), *The New American Bible* (1970), *The New English Bible* (1970), the *New American Standard Bible* (1971), the *Good News Bible: Today's English Version* (1976), the New International Version (1978), the New King James Version (1982), *The New Jerusalem Bible* (1985), *Tanakh: The Holy Scriptures* (new Jewish Publication Society translation, 1985), *The Revised English Bible* (1989), and the New Revised Standard Version (1989). In addition, numerous scholars have produced translations of the Song of Songs, independent of the rest of the Bible. While most of these versions make gestures to indicate that the original is verse, primarily by breaking the text into sections and lines, they tend to lack what poets call "Language"—linguistic and aesthetic qualities, such as poetic texture and density, that mark a text as genuine poetry. Hence the need to go one step further, to combine scholarship with conscious poetic craft and sensibility. This translation is an attempt to fill that need.

I was aware from the outset of the great impact that the King James Version has had on the ears of English readers. Rather than try to echo its rhythms or diction, I set out to

create an entirely fresh version that would open the locked
gardens of the Hebrew. My aim was to probe the roots of the
original and uncover resonances lost in other translations,
but *not* to "Hebraize" English or mimic the aesthetic tech-
niques of Hebrew verse. Rather than writing "transla-
tionese," I tried to write the best poetry I could.

All translations are, by necessity, interpretations. My
interpretations are based on linguistic investigations and literary analysis, which are discussed in the translator's study
that constitutes the second half of this book. Chapter 1 of
this study presents a way of thinking about literary translation and explains my approach to translating the Song; chapter 2 presents the advantages of viewing the Song as a
collection rather than as a structural unity, and explains the
principles behind my reconstruction of the text. Chapters 3,
4, and 5 probe other literary questions relevant to the structure and content of the Song, and chapter 6 treats selected
matters of interpretation in the individual poems. The entire
study focuses on aspects of the text that revealed themselves
in the process of translation; for that reason, reference is
made as needed to both the Hebrew text and the English
renditions. For the reader who knows no Hebrew, word-for-
word translations are provided whenever the Hebrew is cited
and its meaning is not apparent from the context. All Hebrew words in the study are presented in transliterated form,
so that the reader may sense their shapes and sounds. Because of the specific focus of this work, many issues normally
treated by Bible scholars, such as the origin and authorship
of the text, its time of composition, original life setting, and
liturgical functions, are barely touched upon here. Discussions of such issues may be found in the Bible introductions
and commentaries listed in the bibliography.

As I explain in the first chapter of the translator's study,
there can be no truly literal translation of a literary work. Although none of my translations even strives to be literal, all
are attempts to draw close to the meanings, intentions, and
spirit of the original. My aim has been fidelity—not to isolated images, but to the meanings of images in their original

Preface cultural contexts and to the effects they might have had on their earliest audience. Thus, at times, my renditions will seem to depart radically from other, more literal versions.

For example, in chapter 1, verse 9, of the Hebrew (the opening lines of my poem 4), a woman is compared to a mare in Pharaoh's chariotry—a puzzling image, for only stallions, never mares, drew chariots. But the Egyptians' enemies set mares loose in war to drive the pharaoh's stallions wild, and this is the crux of the metaphor. The woman is not simply a beautiful creature; she is as alluring as "a mare among stallions." Seen this way, the image is striking and perhaps even daunting: the beloved possesses a captivating power over her admirer. Yet his response is not to withdraw but to draw nearer; wanting to share love, he offers to adorn the beloved with his own gifts.

The poems in this book are a gift back to their source and an attempt to share in the tradition.

Key to the Biblical Text

---

*6:12 of the Hebrew has not been translated because its meaning is not decipherable, but it has been presented at the bottom of the page on which the Hebrew poem 21 appears.

Masoretic corrections are found in the margins of the Hebrew poems 6, 9, and 17.

Key to the Typefaces
in the English Poems

In the English poems, roman type indicates that a female voice is speaking; *italic* type indicates that a male voice is speaking; SMALL CAPITALS indicate that an unidentifiable voice or a group of voices is speaking.

❧

When a poem continues beyond a page, it does so after a stanza break.

THE SONG OF SONGS

THIRTY-ONE LYRIC POEMS
IN HEBREW AND IN
ENGLISH TRANSLATION

שִׁיר הַשִּׁירִים אֲשֶׁר לִשְׁלֹמֹה׃

The Song of Songs

א

יִשָּׁקֵנִי מִנְּשִׁיקוֹת פִּיהוּ
כִּי־טוֹבִים דֹּדֶיךָ מִיָּיִן:
לְרֵיחַ שְׁמָנֶיךָ טוֹבִים
שֶׁמֶן תּוּרַק שְׁמֶךָ
עַל־כֵּן עֲלָמוֹת אֲהֵבוּךָ:

מָשְׁכֵנִי אַחֲרֶיךָ נָּרוּצָה
הֱבִיאַנִי הַמֶּלֶךְ חֲדָרָיו
נָגִילָה וְנִשְׂמְחָה בָּךְ
נַזְכִּירָה דֹדֶיךָ מִיַּיִן
מֵישָׁרִים אֲהֵבוּךָ:

❧ I

O for your kiss! For your love
More enticing than wine,
For your scent and sweet name—
For all this they love you.

Take me away to your room,
Like a king to his rooms—
We'll rejoice there with wine.
No wonder they love you!

ב

שְׁחוֹרָה אֲנִי וְנָאוָה
בְּנוֹת יְרוּשָׁלַ‍ם
כְּאׇהֳלֵי קֵדָר
כִּירִיעוֹת שְׁלֹמֹה:

אַל־תִּרְאוּנִי שֶׁאֲנִי שְׁחַרְחֹרֶת
שֶׁשֱּׁזָפַתְנִי הַשָּׁמֶשׁ

בְּנֵי אִמִּי נִחֲרוּ־בִי
שָׂמֻנִי נֹטֵרָה אֶת־הַכְּרָמִים
כַּרְמִי שֶׁלִּי לֹא נָטָרְתִּי:

ॐ 2

Yes, I am black! and radiant—
O city women watching me—
As black as Kedar's goathair tents
Or Solomon's fine tapestries.

Will you disrobe me with your stares?
The eyes of many morning suns
Have pierced my skin, and now I shine
Black as the light before the dawn.

And I have faced the angry glare
Of others, even my mother's sons
Who sent me out to watch their vines
While I neglected all my own.

‏ג ‏

הַגִּידָה לִּי שֶׁאָהֲבָה֙ נַפְשִׁי
אֵיכָ֣ה תִרְעֶ֔ה
אֵיכָ֖ה תַּרְבִּ֣יץ בַּֽצָּהֳרָ֑יִם
שַׁלָּמָ֤ה אֶֽהְיֶה֙ כְּעֹ֣טְיָ֔ה
עַ֖ל עֶדְרֵ֥י חֲבֵרֶֽיךָ׃

אִם־לֹ֤א תֵֽדְעִי֙ לָ֔ךְ
הַיָּפָ֖ה בַּנָּשִׁ֑ים
צְֽאִי־לָ֞ךְ בְּעִקְבֵ֣י הַצֹּ֗אן
וּרְעִי֙ אֶת־גְּדִיֹּתַ֔יִךְ
עַ֖ל מִשְׁכְּנ֥וֹת הָרֹעִֽים׃

ᔆᔆ 3

Tell me, my love, where you feed your sheep
And where you rest in the afternoon,
For why should I go searching blindly
Among the flocks of your friends?

If you don't know, O lovely woman,
Follow the tracks that the sheep have made
And feed your own little goats and lambs
In the fields where the shepherds lie.

ד 8≤

לְסֻסָתִי בְּרִכְבֵי פַרְעֹה
דִּמִּיתִיךְ רַעְיָתִי:

נָאווּ לְחָיַיִךְ בַּתֹּרִים
צַוָּארֵךְ בַּחֲרוּזִים:

תּוֹרֵי זָהָב נַעֲשֶׂה־לָּךְ
עִם נְקֻדּוֹת הַכָּסֶף:

ই৶ 4

Like a mare among stallions,
You lure, I am held

> *your cheeks framed with braids*
> *your neck traced with shells*

I'll adorn you with gold
And with silver bells

לְסֻסָתִי בְּרִכְבֵי פַרְעֹה
דִּמִּיתִיךְ רַעְיָתִי

෴

Like a mare among stallions,
You lure, I am held

ה ⇜

עַד־שֶׁהַמֶּ֫לֶךְ֙ בִּמְסִבּ֔וֹ
נִרְדִּ֖י נָתַ֥ן רֵיחֽוֹ׃

צְר֨וֹר הַמֹּ֤ר ׀ דּוֹדִי֙ לִ֔י
בֵּ֥ין שָׁדַ֖י יָלִֽין׃

אֶשְׁכֹּ֨ל הַכֹּ֤פֶר ׀ דּוֹדִי֙ לִ֔י
בְּכַרְמֵ֖י עֵ֥ין גֶּֽדִי׃

ૐ 5

Until the king returns
    I lie in fragrance,
Sweet anticipation
    Of his entrance.

Between my breasts he'll lie—
    Sachet of spices,
Spray of blossoms plucked
    From the oasis.

‎ו ‎&

הִנָּךְ יָפָה רַעְיָתִי
הִנָּךְ יָפָה
עֵינַיִךְ יוֹנִים:

הִנְּךָ יָפֶה דוֹדִי
אַף נָעִים
אַף־עַרְשֵׂנוּ רַעֲנָנָה:
קֹרוֹת בָּתֵּינוּ אֲרָזִים
*רַחִיטֵנוּ בְּרוֹתִים:

*רַהִיטֵנוּ

≥● 6

How fine
you are, my love,
your eyes
like doves'.

How fine
are you, my lover,
what joy
we have together.

How green
our bed of leaves,
our rafters of cedars,
our juniper eaves.

ב ‎8ح

אֲנִי חֲבַצֶּלֶת הַשָּׁרוֹן
שׁוֹשַׁנַּת הָעֲמָקִים:

כְּשׁוֹשַׁנָּה בֵּין הַחוֹחִים
כֵּן רַעְיָתִי בֵּין הַבָּנוֹת:

כְּתַפּוּחַ בַּעֲצֵי הַיַּעַר
כֵּן דּוֹדִי בֵּין הַבָּנִים
בְּצִלּוֹ חִמַּדְתִּי וְיָשַׁבְתִּי
וּפִרְיוֹ מָתוֹק לְחִכִּי:

❧ 7

In sandy earth or deep
In valley soil
I grow, a wildflower thriving
On your love.

Narcissus in the brambles,
Brightest flower—
I choose you from all others
For my love.

Sweet fruit tree growing wild
Within the thickets—
I blossom in your shade
And taste your love.

ח ‏אי

הֱבִיאַ֙נִי֙ אֶל־בֵּ֣ית הַיַּ֔יִן
וְדִגְל֥וֹ עָלַ֖י אַהֲבָֽה׃

סַמְּכ֙וּנִי֙ בָּֽאֲשִׁישׁ֔וֹת
רַפְּד֖וּנִי בַּתַּפּוּחִ֑ים
כִּי־חוֹלַ֥ת אַהֲבָ֖ה אָֽנִי׃

שְׂמֹאלוֹ֙ תַּ֣חַת לְרֹאשִׁ֔י
וִימִינ֖וֹ תְּחַבְּקֵֽנִי׃

הִשְׁבַּ֙עְתִּי אֶתְכֶ֜ם בְּנ֤וֹת יְרוּשָׁלִַ֙ם֙
בִּצְבָא֔וֹת א֖וֹ בְּאַיְל֣וֹת הַשָּׂדֶ֑ה
אִם־תָּעִ֧ירוּ ׀ וְֽאִם־תְּע֛וֹרְר֛וּ
אֶת־הָאַהֲבָ֖ה עַ֥ד שֶׁתֶּחְפָּֽץ׃

ஃ 8

He brings me to the winehall,
Gazing at me with love.

Feed me raisincakes and quinces!
For I am sick with love.

O for his arms around me,
Beneath me and above!

O women of the city,
Swear by the wild field doe

Not to wake or rouse us
Till we fulfill our love.

ט *

קוֹל דּוֹדִי הִנֵּה־זֶה בָּא
מְדַלֵּג עַל־הֶהָרִים
מְקַפֵּץ עַל־הַגְּבָעוֹת:
דּוֹמֶה דוֹדִי לִצְבִי
אוֹ לְעֹפֶר הָאַיָּלִים
הִנֵּה־זֶה עוֹמֵד אַחַר כָּתְלֵנוּ
מַשְׁגִּיחַ מִן־הַחַלֹּנוֹת
מֵצִיץ מִן־הַחֲרַכִּים:

עָנָה דוֹדִי וְאָמַר לִי

קוּמִי לָךְ רַעְיָתִי
יָפָתִי וּלְכִי־לָךְ:

כִּי־הִנֵּה *הַסְּתָו עָבָר *הַסְּתָיו
הַגֶּשֶׁם חָלַף הָלַךְ לוֹ:
הַנִּצָּנִים נִרְאוּ בָאָרֶץ
עֵת הַזָּמִיר הִגִּיעַ
וְקוֹל הַתּוֹר נִשְׁמַע בְּאַרְצֵנוּ:
הַתְּאֵנָה חָנְטָה פַגֶּיהָ
וְהַגְּפָנִים | סְמָדַר נָתְנוּ רֵיחַ

קוּמִי *לְכִי רַעְיָתִי *לָךְ
יָפָתִי וּלְכִי־לָךְ:

ॐ 9

The sound of my lover
coming from the hills
quickly, like a deer
upon the mountains

Now at my windows,
walking by the walls,
here at the lattices
he calls—

Come with me,
my love,
come away

For the long wet months are past,
the rains have fed the earth
and left it bright with blossoms

Birds wing in the low sky,
dove and songbird singing
in the open air above

Earth nourishing tree and vine,
green fig and tender grape,
green and tender fragrance

Come with me,
my love,
come away

י ‎🙐

יוֹנָתִי בְּחַגְוֵי הַסֶּלַע
בְּסֵתֶר הַמַּדְרֵגָה
הַרְאִינִי אֶת־מַרְאַיִךְ
הַשְׁמִיעִנִי אֶת־קוֹלֵךְ
כִּי־קוֹלֵךְ עָרֵב
וּמַרְאֵיךְ נָאוֶה:

৵ 10

My dove
      in the clefts
            of the rocks
      the secret
            of steep ravines

Come let me look at you
Come let me hear you

      Your voice clear as water
      Your beautiful body

יוֹנָתִי בְּחַגְוֵי הַסֶּלַע
בְּסֵתֶר הַמַּדְרֵגָה

&

My dove
in the clefts
of the rocks

אֶחֱזוּ־לָנוּ שׁוּעָלִים
שׁוּעָלִים קְטַנִּים
מְחַבְּלִים כְּרָמִים
וּכְרָמֵינוּ סְמָדַר:

෫ II

CATCH THE FOXES!
    THE LITTLE FOXES
    AMONG THE VINES
CATCH THE FOXES!
    THE QUICK LITTLE FOXES
    RAIDING THE NEW GRAPES
    ON OUR VINES

יב ₪

דּוֹדִי לִי וַאֲנִי לוֹ
הָרֹעֶה בַּשּׁוֹשַׁנִּים:

עַד שֶׁיָּפוּחַ הַיּוֹם
וְנָסוּ הַצְּלָלִים
סֹב דְּמֵה־לְךָ
דוֹדִי לִצְבִי
אוֹ לְעֹפֶר הָאַיָּלִים
עַל־הָרֵי בָתֶר:

੪ 12

My lover turns to me,
I turn to him,
Who leads his flock to feed
Among the flowers.

Until the day is over
And the shadows flee,
Turn round, my lover,
Go quickly, and be
Like deer or gazelles
In the clefts of the hills.

יג ‏8

עַל־מִשְׁכָּבִי בַּלֵּילוֹת
בִּקַּשְׁתִּי אֵת שֶׁאָהֲבָה נַפְשִׁי
בִּקַּשְׁתִּיו וְלֹא מְצָאתִיו:

אָקוּמָה נָּא וַאֲסוֹבְבָה בָעִיר
בַּשְּׁוָקִים וּבָרְחֹבוֹת
אֲבַקְשָׁה אֵת שֶׁאָהֲבָה נַפְשִׁי
בִּקַּשְׁתִּיו וְלֹא מְצָאתִיו:

מְצָאוּנִי הַשֹּׁמְרִים הַסֹּבְבִים בָּעִיר
אֵת שֶׁאָהֲבָה נַפְשִׁי רְאִיתֶם:
כִּמְעַט שֶׁעָבַרְתִּי מֵהֶם
עַד שֶׁמָּצָאתִי אֵת שֶׁאָהֲבָה נַפְשִׁי

אֲחַזְתִּיו וְלֹא אַרְפֶּנּוּ
עַד־שֶׁהֲבֵיאתִיו אֶל־בֵּית אִמִּי
וְאֶל־חֶדֶר הוֹרָתִי:

הִשְׁבַּעְתִּי אֶתְכֶם בְּנוֹת יְרוּשָׁלַם
בִּצְבָאוֹת אוֹ בְּאַיְלוֹת הַשָּׂדֶה
אִם־תָּעִירוּ ׀ וְאִם־תְּעוֹרְרוּ
אֶת־הָאַהֲבָה עַד שֶׁתֶּחְפָּץ:

❧ 13

At night in bed, I want him—
The one I love is not here.

I'll rise and search the city,
Through the streets and squares

Until the city watchmen
Find me wandering there

And I ask them—have you seen him?
The one I love is not here.

When they have gone, I find him
And I won't let him go

Until he's in my mother's home,
The room where I was born.

O women of the city,
Swear by the wild field doe

Not to wake or rouse us
Till we fulfill our love.

יד ⁌

מִי זֹאת עֹלָה֙ מִן־הַמִּדְבָּ֔ר
כְּתִימֲרוֹת עָשָׁ֑ן
מְקֻטֶּ֤רֶת מוֹר֙ וּלְבוֹנָ֔ה
מִכֹּ֖ל אַבְקַ֥ת רוֹכֵֽל:

הִנֵּ֗ה מִטָּתוֹ֙ שֶׁלִּשְׁלֹמֹ֔ה
שִׁשִּׁ֥ים גִּבֹּרִ֖ים סָבִ֣יב לָ֑הּ
מִגִּבֹּרֵ֖י יִשְׂרָאֵֽל:
כֻּלָּם֙ אֲחֻ֣זֵי חֶ֔רֶב
מְלֻמְּדֵ֖י מִלְחָמָ֑ה
אִ֤ישׁ חַרְבּוֹ֙ עַל־יְרֵכ֔וֹ
מִפַּ֖חַד בַּלֵּילֽוֹת:

אַפִּרְי֗וֹן עָ֤שָׂה לוֹ֙
הַמֶּ֣לֶךְ שְׁלֹמֹ֔ה
מֵעֲצֵ֖י הַלְּבָנֽוֹן:
עַמּוּדָיו֙ עָ֣שָׂה כֶ֔סֶף
רְפִידָת֣וֹ זָהָ֔ב
מֶרְכָּב֖וֹ אַרְגָּמָ֑ן
תּוֹכוֹ֙ רָצ֣וּף אַהֲבָ֔ה
מִבְּנ֖וֹת יְרוּשָׁלָֽם:

צְאֶ֧ינָה ׀ וּרְאֶ֛ינָה בְּנ֥וֹת צִיּ֖וֹן
בַּמֶּ֣לֶךְ שְׁלֹמֹ֑ה
בָּעֲטָרָ֗ה שֶׁעִטְּרָה־לּ֤וֹ אִמּוֹ֙
בְּי֣וֹם חֲתֻנָּת֔וֹ
וּבְי֖וֹם שִׂמְחַ֥ת לִבּֽוֹ:

ह14

WHO IS THIS APPROACHING, UP FROM THE DESERT
IN COLUMNS OF SMOKE, FRAGRANT WITH INCENSE,
RARE SPICES AND HERBS OF THE WANDERING MERCHANTS?

BEHOLD, IT APPEARS—THE KING'S OWN PROCESSION
ATTENDED BY SIXTY OF ISRAEL'S WARRIORS,
SWORDS AT THEIR THIGHS TO MEET THE NIGHT'S DANGERS.

A CARRIAGE OF CEDAR WITH PILLARS OF SILVER,
GOLD FLOOR, PURPLE CUSHIONS, ALL MADE TO HIS ORDERS
AND FASHIONED WITH LOVE BY JERUSALEM'S DAUGHTERS.

GO OUT AND SEE, O JERUSALEM'S DAUGHTERS!
CROWNED BY HIS MOTHER, THE KING IN HIS CARRIAGE
THIS DAY OF REJOICING, THIS DAY OF HIS MARRIAGE.

טו

הִנָּךְ יָפָה רַעְיָתִי
הִנָּךְ יָפָה
עֵינַיִךְ יוֹנִים
מִבַּעַד לְצַמָּתֵךְ

שַׂעְרֵךְ כְּעֵדֶר הָעִזִּים
שֶׁגָּלְשׁוּ מֵהַר גִּלְעָד:

שִׁנַּיִךְ כְּעֵדֶר הַקְּצוּבוֹת
שֶׁעָלוּ מִן־הָרַחְצָה
שֶׁכֻּלָּם מַתְאִימוֹת
וְשַׁכֻּלָה אֵין בָּהֶם:

כְּחוּט הַשָּׁנִי שִׂפְתוֹתַיִךְ
וּמִדְבָּרֵךְ נָאוֶה

כְּפֶלַח הָרִמּוֹן רַקָּתֵךְ
מִבַּעַד לְצַמָּתֵךְ:

כְּמִגְדַּל דָּוִיד צַוָּארֵךְ
בָּנוּי לְתַלְפִּיּוֹת
אֶלֶף הַמָּגֵן תָּלוּי עָלָיו
כֹּל שִׁלְטֵי הַגִּבּוֹרִים:

שְׁנֵי שָׁדַיִךְ כִּשְׁנֵי עֳפָרִים
תְּאוֹמֵי צְבִיָּה
הָרוֹעִים בַּשּׁוֹשַׁנִּים:

❧ 15

How fine
you are, my love,
your eyes like doves'
behind your veil

Your hair—
as black as goats
winding down the slopes

Your teeth—
a flock of sheep
rising from the stream
in twos, each with its twin

Your lips—
like woven threads
of crimson silk

A gleam of pomegranate—
your forehead
through your veil

Your neck—
a tower
adorned with shields

Your breasts—
twin fawns
in fields of flowers

עַד שֶׁיָּפ֫וּחַ� הַיּ֔וֹם
וְנָ֫סוּ הַצְּלָלִ֑ים
אֵלֶךְ לִי֙ אֶל־הַ֣ר הַמּ֔וֹר
וְאֶל־גִּבְעַ֖ת הַלְּבוֹנָֽה׃

כֻּלָּ֤ךְ יָפָה֙ רַעְיָתִ֔י
וּמ֖וּם אֵ֥ין בָּֽךְ׃

Until
the day is over,
shadows gone,

I'll go
up to the hills
of fragrant bloom

How fine
you are, my love,
my perfect one

טז &

אִתִּי מִלְּבָנוֹן֙ כַּלָּ֔ה
אִתִּי מִלְּבָנ֖וֹן תָּב֑וֹאִי
תָּשׁ֡וּרִי ׀ מֵרֹ֣אשׁ אֲמָנָ֗ה
מֵרֹ֤אשׁ שְׂנִיר֙ וְחֶרְמ֔וֹן
מִמְּעֹנ֣וֹת אֲרָי֔וֹת
מֵהַרְרֵ֖י נְמֵרִֽים׃

ᢞ 16

With me, my bride of the mountains,
Come away with me, come away!

Come down from the peaks of the mountains,
From the perilous Lebanon caves,

From the lairs where lions crouch hidden,
Where leopards watch nightly for prey,

Look down, look down and come away!

מִמְּעֹנוֹת אֲרָיוֹת
מֵהַרְרֵי נְמֵרִים

&

From the lairs where lions crouch hidden,
Where leopards watch nightly for prey

לִבַּבְתִּנִי אֲחֹתִי כַלָּה

לִבַּבְתִּ֫נִי֙ *בְּאַחַד מֵעֵינַ֫יִךְ   *בְּאַחַת

בְּאַחַד עֲנָק מִצַּוְּרֹנָֽיִךְ:

מַה־יָּפוּ דֹדַ֫יִךְ אֲחֹתִי כַלָּה

מַה־טֹּבוּ דֹדַ֫יִךְ֙ מִיַּ֫יִן

וְרֵ֫יחַ שְׁמָנַ֫יִךְ מִכָּל־בְּשָׂמִֽים:

נֹ֫פֶת תִּטֹּ֫פְנָה שִׂפְתוֹתַ֫יִךְ כַּלָּה

דְּבַשׁ וְחָלָב֙ תַּחַת לְשׁוֹנֵ֫ךְ

וְרֵ֫יחַ שַׂלְמֹתַ֫יִךְ כְּרֵ֫יחַ לְבָנֽוֹן:

🐦 17

With one flash of your eyes, you excite me,
One jewel on your neck stirs my heart,
    O my sister, my bride.

Your love, more than wine, is enticing,
Your fragrance is finer than spices,
    My sister, my bride.

Your lips, sweet with nectar, invite me
To honey and milk on your tongue,
    O my sister, my bride.

And even your clothing is fragrant
As wind from the Lebanon mountains,
    My sister, my bride.

‏יח‎ ‏&‎

גַּן ׀ נָעוּל אֲחֹתִי כַלָּה
גַּל נָעוּל מַעְיָן חָתוּם:
שְׁלָחַיִךְ פַּרְדֵּס רִמּוֹנִים
עִם פְּרִי מְגָדִים
כְּפָרִים עִם־נְרָדִים:
נֵרְדְּ ׀ וְכַרְכֹּם קָנֶה וְקִנָּמוֹן
עִם כָּל־עֲצֵי לְבוֹנָה
מֹר וַאֲהָלוֹת
עִם כָּל־רָאשֵׁי בְשָׂמִים:
מַעְיַן גַּנִּים
בְּאֵר מַיִם חַיִּים
וְנֹזְלִים מִן־לְבָנוֹן:

עוּרִי צָפוֹן וּבוֹאִי תֵימָן
הָפִיחִי גַנִּי יִזְּלוּ בְשָׂמָיו
יָבֹא דוֹדִי לְגַנּוֹ
וְיֹאכַל פְּרִי מְגָדָיו:

בָּאתִי לְגַנִּי אֲחֹתִי כַלָּה
אָרִיתִי מוֹרִי עִם־בְּשָׂמִי
אָכַלְתִּי יַעְרִי עִם־דִּבְשִׁי
שָׁתִיתִי יֵינִי עִם־חֲלָבִי

אִכְלוּ רֵעִים
שְׁתוּ וְשִׁכְרוּ דּוֹדִים:

৯ 18

Enclosed and hidden, you are a garden,
A still pool, a fountain.

Stretching your limbs, you open—
A field of pomegranates blooms,

Treasured fruit among the blossoms,
Henna, sweet cane, bark, and saffron,

Fragrant woods and succulents,
The finest spices and perfumes.

Living water, you are a fountain,
A well, a river flowing from the mountains.

Come, north winds and south winds!
Breathe upon my garden,

Bear its fragrance to my lover,
Let him come and share its treasures.

My bride, my sister, I have come
To gather spices in my garden,

To taste wild honey with my wine,
Milk and honey with my wine.

FEAST, DRINK—AND DRINK DEEPLY—LOVERS!

יט ‏

אֲנִי יְשֵׁנָה וְלִבִּי עֵר
קוֹל ׀ דּוֹדִי דוֹפֵק

פִּתְחִי־לִּי אֲחֹתִי רַעְיָתִי
יוֹנָתִי תַמָּתִי
שֶׁרֹּאשִׁי נִמְלָא־טָל
קְוֻצּוֹתַי רְסִיסֵי לָיְלָה:

פָּשַׁטְתִּי אֶת־כֻּתָּנְתִּי
אֵיכָכָה אֶלְבָּשֶׁנָּה
רָחַצְתִּי אֶת־רַגְלַי
אֵיכָכָה אֲטַנְּפֵם:

דּוֹדִי שָׁלַח יָדוֹ מִן־הַחֹר
וּמֵעַי הָמוּ עָלָיו:

קַמְתִּי אֲנִי לִפְתֹּחַ לְדוֹדִי
וְיָדַי נָטְפוּ־מוֹר
וְאֶצְבְּעֹתַי מוֹר עֹבֵר
עַל כַּפּוֹת הַמַּנְעוּל:

פָּתַחְתִּי אֲנִי לְדוֹדִי
וְדוֹדִי חָמַק עָבָר

נַפְשִׁי יָצְאָה בְדַבְּרוֹ
בִּקַּשְׁתִּיהוּ וְלֹא מְצָאתִיהוּ
קְרָאתִיו וְלֹא עָנָנִי:

מְצָאֻנִי הַשֹּׁמְרִים הַסֹּבְבִים בָּעִיר
הִכּוּנִי פְצָעוּנִי
נָשְׂאוּ אֶת־רְדִידִי מֵעָלַי
שֹׁמְרֵי הַחֹמוֹת:

ॐ 19

I sleep, but my heart stirs,
restless,
              and dreams . . .

My lover's voice here, at the door—

Open, my love, my sister,
my dove, my perfect one,
for my hair is soaked with the night.

Should I get up, get dressed,
and dirty my feet?

My love thrusts his hand at the latch
and my heart leaps for him!

I rise to open for my love,
my hands dripping perfume on the lock—

I open,
but he has gone.

I run out after him, calling,
but he is gone.

The men who roam the streets,
guarding the walls,
beat me and tear away my robe.

הִשְׁבַּעְתִּי אֶתְכֶם בְּנוֹת יְרוּשָׁלָ֫ם
אִם־תִּמְצְאוּ֙ אֶת־דּוֹדִ֔י
מַה־תַּגִּ֣ידוּ ל֔וֹ
שֶׁחוֹלַ֥ת אַהֲבָ֖ה אָֽנִי׃

מַה־דּוֹדֵ֣ךְ מִדּ֔וֹד
הַיָּפָ֖ה בַּנָּשִׁ֑ים
מַה־דּוֹדֵ֣ךְ מִדּ֔וֹד
שֶׁכָּ֖כָה הִשְׁבַּעְתָּֽנוּ׃

דּוֹדִ֥י צַח֙ וְאָד֔וֹם
דָּג֖וּל מֵרְבָבָֽה׃

רֹאשׁ֖וֹ כֶּ֣תֶם פָּ֑ז
קְוֻּצּוֹתָיו֙ תַּלְתַּלִּ֔ים
שְׁחֹר֖וֹת כָּעוֹרֵֽב׃

עֵינָ֕יו כְּיוֹנִ֖ים
עַל־אֲפִ֣יקֵי מָ֑יִם
רֹֽחֲצוֹת֙ בֶּֽחָלָ֔ב
יֹשְׁב֖וֹת עַל־מִלֵּֽאת׃

לְחָיָו֙ כַּעֲרוּגַ֣ת הַבֹּ֔שֶׂם
מִגְדְּל֖וֹת מֶרְקָחִ֑ים
שִׂפְתוֹתָיו֙ שֽׁוֹשַׁנִּ֔ים
נֹטְפ֖וֹת מ֥וֹר עֹבֵֽר׃

יָדָיו֙ גְּלִילֵ֣י זָהָ֔ב
מְמֻלָּאִ֖ים בַּתַּרְשִׁ֑ישׁ
מֵעָיו֙ עֶ֣שֶׁת שֵׁ֔ן
מְעֻלֶּ֖פֶת סַפִּירִֽים׃

O women of the city,
Swear to me!
If you find my lover
You will say
That I am sick with love.

WHO IS YOUR LOVE
AND WHY DO YOU BIND US BY OATH?

My love is radiant
As gold or crimson,
Hair in waves of black
Like wings of ravens.

Eyes like doves, afloat
Upon the water,
Bathed in milk, at rest
On brimming pools.

Cheeks like beds of spices,
Banks of flowers,
Lips like lilies, sweet
And wet with dew.

Studded with jewels, his arms
Are round and golden,
His belly smooth as ivory,
Bright with gems.

שׁוֹקָיו֙ עַמּ֣וּדֵי שֵׁ֔שׁ
מְיֻסָּדִ֖ים עַל־אַדְנֵי־פָ֑ז

מַרְאֵ֙הוּ֙ כַּלְּבָנ֔וֹן
בָּח֖וּר כָּאֲרָזִֽים׃

חִכּוֹ֙ מַֽמְתַקִּ֔ים
וְכֻלּ֖וֹ מַחֲמַדִּ֑ים

זֶ֤ה דוֹדִי֙ וְזֶ֣ה רֵעִ֔י
בְּנ֖וֹת יְרוּשָׁלָֽ͏ִם׃

אָ֚נָה הָלַ֣ךְ דּוֹדֵ֔ךְ
הַיָּפָ֖ה בַּנָּשִׁ֑ים
אָ֚נָה פָּנָ֣ה דוֹדֵ֔ךְ
וּנְבַקְשֶׁ֖נּוּ עִמָּֽךְ׃

דּוֹדִי֙ יָרַ֣ד לְגַנּ֔וֹ
לַעֲרוּג֖וֹת הַבֹּ֑שֶׂם
לִרְעוֹת֙ בַּגַּנִּ֔ים
וְלִלְקֹ֖ט שֽׁוֹשַׁנִּֽים׃

אֲנִ֤י לְדוֹדִי֙ וְדוֹדִ֣י לִ֔י
הָרֹעֶ֖ה בַּשּֽׁוֹשַׁנִּֽים׃

Set in gold, his legs,
Two marble columns—
He stands as proud as cedars
In the mountains.

Man of pleasure—sweet
To taste his love!
Friend and lover chosen
For my love.

BEAUTIFUL WOMAN,
WHERE HAS YOUR LOVER GONE TO?
WHERE HAS HE GONE?
WE'LL HELP YOU LOOK FOR HIM.

My love has gone to walk
Within his garden—
To feed his sheep and there
To gather flowers.

I turn to meet my love,
He'll turn to me,
Who leads his flock to feed
Among the flowers.

קְוֻצּוֹתָיו תַּלְתַּלִּים
שְׁחֹרוֹת כָּעוֹרֵב

৯

Hair in waves of black
Like wings of ravens

יָפָה אַתְּ רַעְיָתִי כְּתִרְצָה
נָאוָה כִּירוּשָׁלָ͏ִם
אֲיֻמָּה כַּנִּדְגָּלוֹת:
הָסֵבִּי עֵינַיִךְ מִנֶּגְדִּי
שֶׁהֵם הִרְהִיבֻנִי

שַׂעְרֵךְ כְּעֵדֶר הָעִזִּים
שֶׁגָּלְשׁוּ מִן־הַגִּלְעָד:
שִׁנַּיִךְ כְּעֵדֶר הָרְחֵלִים
שֶׁעָלוּ מִן־הָרַחְצָה
שֶׁכֻּלָּם מַתְאִימוֹת
וְשַׁכֻּלָה אֵין בָּהֶם:
כְּפֶלַח הָרִמּוֹן רַקָּתֵךְ
מִבַּעַד לְצַמָּתֵךְ:

שִׁשִּׁים הֵמָּה מְלָכוֹת
וּשְׁמֹנִים פִּילַגְשִׁים
וַעֲלָמוֹת אֵין מִסְפָּר:
אַחַת הִיא יוֹנָתִי תַמָּתִי
אַחַת הִיא לְאִמָּהּ
בָּרָה הִיא לְיוֹלַדְתָּהּ
רָאוּהָ בָנוֹת וַיְאַשְּׁרוּהָ
מְלָכוֹת וּפִילַגְשִׁים וַיְהַלְלוּהָ:

מִי־זֹאת הַנִּשְׁקָפָה כְּמוֹ־שָׁחַר
יָפָה כַלְּבָנָה
בָּרָה כַּחַמָּה
אֲיֻמָּה כַּנִּדְגָּלוֹת:

ล๏ 20

Striking as Tirza
    you are, my love,
Bright as Jerusalem,
    frightening as visions!
Lower your eyes
    for they make me tremble

Your hair—as black as goats
    winding down the slopes
Your teeth—a flock of sheep
    rising from the stream
    in twos, each with its twin
A gleam of pomegranate—
    your forehead through your veil

Sixty queens, eighty brides,
    endless numbers of women—
One is my dove, my perfect one,
    pure as an only child—
Women see her
    and sing of her joy,
Queens and brides
    chant her praise

Who is she? staring
    down like the dawn's eye,
Bright as the white moon,
    pure as the hot sun,
Frightening as visions!

כא

אֶל־גִּנַּת אֱגוֹז יָרַדְתִּי
לִרְאוֹת בְּאִבֵּי הַנָּחַל
לִרְאוֹת הֲפָרְחָה הַגֶּפֶן
הֵנֵצוּ הָרִמֹּנִים:

לֹא יָדַעְתִּי נַפְשִׁי שָׂמַתְנִי מַרְכְּבוֹת עַמִּי־נָדִיב:

ஃ 21

Walking through the walnut orchard,
Looking for the signs of spring:
The pomegranates—have they flowered?
The grapevines—are they blossoming?

‏‮כב‬ ‮&‬

שׁוּבִי שׁוּבִי הַשּׁוּלַמִּית
שׁוּבִי שׁוּבִי וְנֶחֱזֶה־בָּךְ

מַה־תֶּחֱזוּ בַּשּׁוּלַמִּית
כִּמְחֹלַת הַמַּחֲנָיִם:

מַה־יָּפוּ פְעָמַיִךְ
בַּנְּעָלִים בַּת־נָדִיב

חַמּוּקֵי יְרֵכַיִךְ כְּמוֹ חֲלָאִים
מַעֲשֵׂה יְדֵי אָמָּן:

שָׁרְרֵךְ אַגַּן הַסַּהַר
אַל־יֶחְסַר הַמָּזֶג

בִּטְנֵךְ עֲרֵמַת חִטִּים
סוּגָה בַּשּׁוֹשַׁנִּים:

שְׁנֵי שָׁדַיִךְ כִּשְׁנֵי עֳפָרִים
תָּאֳמֵי צְבִיָּה:

צַוָּארֵךְ כְּמִגְדַּל הַשֵּׁן

עֵינַיִךְ בְּרֵכוֹת בְּחֶשְׁבּוֹן
עַל־שַׁעַר בַּת־רַבִּים

אַפֵּךְ כְּמִגְדַּל הַלְּבָנוֹן
צוֹפֶה פְּנֵי דַמָּשֶׂק:

רֹאשֵׁךְ עָלַיִךְ כַּכַּרְמֶל
וְדַלַּת רֹאשֵׁךְ כָּאַרְגָּמָן
מֶלֶךְ אָסוּר בָּרְהָטִים:

ào 22

DANCE FOR US, PRINCESS, DANCE,
    AS WE WATCH AND CHANT!

What will you see as I move
    in the dance of love?

YOUR GRACEFUL, SANDALLED FEET,
YOUR THIGHS—TWO SPINNING JEWELS,
YOUR HIPS—A BOWL OF NECTAR
    BRIMMING FULL

YOUR BELLY—GOLDEN WHEAT
ADORNED WITH DAFFODILS,
YOUR BREASTS—TWO FAWNS, THE TWINS
    OF A GAZELLE

YOUR NECK—AN IVORY TOWER,
YOUR EYES—TWO SILENT POOLS,
YOUR FACE—A TOWER THAT OVERLOOKS
    THE HILLS

YOUR HEAD—MAJESTIC MOUNTAIN
CROWNED WITH PURPLE HAIR,
CAPTIVATING KINGS
    WITHIN ITS LOCKS

‮כג‬ ‮&‬

מַה־יָּפִית֙ וּמַה־נָּעַ֔מְתְּ
אַהֲבָ֖ה בַּתַּעֲנוּגִֽים:

זֹ֤את קֽוֹמָתֵךְ֙ דָּֽמְתָ֣ה לְתָמָ֔ר
וְשָׁדַ֖יִךְ לְאַשְׁכֹּלֽוֹת:

אָמַ֙רְתִּי֙ אֶעֱלֶ֣ה בְתָמָ֔ר
אֹֽחֲזָ֖ה בְּסַנְסִנָּ֑יו

וְיִֽהְיוּ־נָ֤א שָׁדַ֙יִךְ֙ כְּאֶשְׁכְּל֣וֹת הַגֶּ֔פֶן
וְרֵ֥יחַ אַפֵּ֖ךְ כַּתַּפּוּחִֽים:

וְחִכֵּ֕ךְ כְּיֵ֥ין הַטּ֖וֹב
הוֹלֵ֥ךְ לְדוֹדִ֖י לְמֵישָׁרִ֑ים
דּוֹבֵ֖ב שִׂפְתֵ֥י יְשֵׁנִֽים:

ஃ 23

Of all pleasure, how sweet
Is the taste of love!

There you stand like a palm,
Your breasts clusters of dates.

Shall I climb that palm
And take hold of the boughs?

Your breasts will be tender
As clusters of grapes,

Your breath will be sweet
As the fragrance of quince,

And your mouth will awaken
All sleeping desire

Like wine that entices
The lips of new lovers.

אָמַרְתִּי אֶעֱלֶה בְתָמָר
אֹחֲזָה בְּסַנְסִנָּיו

❧

Shall I climb that palm
And take hold of the boughs?

כד 8

אֲנִי לְדוֹדִי וְעָלַי תְּשׁוּקָתְו:

לְכָה דוֹדִי נֵצֵא הַשָּׂדֶה
נָלִינָה בַּכְּפָרִים:
נַשְׁכִּימָה לַכְּרָמִים
נִרְאֶה אִם פָּרְחָה הַגֶּפֶן
פִּתַּח הַסְּמָדַר
הֵנֵצוּ הָרִמּוֹנִים

שָׁם אֶתֵּן אֶת־דֹּדַי לָךְ:
הַדּוּדָאִים נָתְנוּ־רֵיחַ
וְעַל־פְּתָחֵינוּ כָּל־מְגָדִים
חֲדָשִׁים גַּם־יְשָׁנִים
דּוֹדִי צָפַנְתִּי לָךְ:

≈ 24

Turning to him, who meets me with desire—

Come, love, let us go out to the open fields
And spend our night lying where the henna blooms,
Rising early to leave for the near vineyards
Where the vines flower, opening tender buds,
And the pomegranate boughs unfold their blossoms.

There among blossom and vine I will give you my love,
Musk of the violet mandrakes spilled upon us . . .
And returning, finding our doorways piled with fruits,
The best of the new-picked and the long-stored,
My love, I will give you all I have saved for you.

‎כה ‏

מִי יִתֶּנְךָ֙ כְּאָ֣ח לִ֔י
יוֹנֵ֖ק שְׁדֵ֣י אִמִּ֑י
אֶֽמְצָאֲךָ֤ בַחוּץ֙ אֶשָּׁ֣קְךָ֔
גַּ֖ם לֹא־יָב֥וּזוּ לִֽי:
אֶנְהָֽגְךָ֗ אֲבִֽיאֲךָ֛
אֶל־בֵּ֥ית אִמִּ֖י
תְּלַמְּדֵ֑נִי
אַשְׁקְךָ֙ מִיַּ֣יִן הָרֶ֔קַח
מֵעֲסִ֖יס רִמֹּנִֽי:

שְׂמֹאלוֹ֙ תַּ֣חַת רֹאשִׁ֔י
וִימִינ֖וֹ תְּחַבְּקֵֽנִי:

הִשְׁבַּ֥עְתִּי אֶתְכֶ֖ם בְּנ֣וֹת יְרוּשָׁלָ֑ם
מַה־תָּעִ֣ירוּ ׀ וּֽמַה־תְּעֹ֥רְרֽוּ
אֶת־הָאַהֲבָ֖ה עַ֥ד שֶׁתֶּחְפָּֽץ:

ð 25

Oh, if you were my brother
Nursed at my mother's breast,

I'd kiss you in the streets
And never suffer scorn.

I'd bring you to my mother's home
(My mother teaches me)

And give you wine and nectar
From my pomegranates.

O for his arms around me,
Beneath me and above!

O women of the city,
Swear by the wild field doe

Not to wake or rouse us
Till we fulfill our love.

‏כו‎ ‎

מִי זֹאת עֹלָה֙ מִן־הַמִּדְבָּ֔ר
מִתְרַפֶּ֖קֶת עַל־דּוֹדָ֑הּ

❧ 26

WHO IS THIS APPROACHING,
    UP FROM THE WILDERNESS,
        ARM ON HER LOVER'S ARM?

כז

תַּחַת הַתַּפּוּחַ עוֹרַרְתִּיךָ
שָׁמָּה חִבְּלַתְךָ אִמֶּךָ
שָׁמָּה חִבְּלָה יְלָדַתְךָ:

ε♣ 27

Under the quince tree
    you woke
    to my touch
there
    where she conceived
    where she who carried
    and bore you
conceived

כח ﻼ

שִׂימֵ֤נִי כַֽחוֹתָם֙ עַל־לִבֶּ֔ךָ
כַּֽחוֹתָם֙ עַל־זְרוֹעֶ֔ךָ

כִּֽי־עַזָּ֤ה כַמָּ֙וֶת֙ אַֽהֲבָ֔ה
קָשָׁ֥ה כִשְׁא֖וֹל קִנְאָ֑ה
רְשָׁפֶ֕יהָ רִשְׁפֵּ֖י אֵ֑שׁ
שַׁלְהֶ֖בֶתְיָֽה:

מַ֣יִם רַבִּ֗ים לֹ֤א יֽוּכְלוּ֙
לְכַבּ֣וֹת אֶת־הָֽאַהֲבָ֔ה
וּנְהָר֖וֹת לֹ֣א יִשְׁטְפ֑וּהָ

אִם־יִתֵּ֨ן אִ֜ישׁ
אֶת־כָּל־ה֤וֹן בֵּיתוֹ֙ בָּֽאַהֲבָ֔ה
בּ֖וֹז יָב֥וּזוּ לֽוֹ:

ೈ 28

Stamp me in your heart,
Upon your limbs,
Sear my emblem deep
Into your skin.

For love is strong as death,
Harsh as the grave.
Its tongues are flames, a fierce
And holy blaze.

Endless seas and floods,
Torrents and rivers
Never put out love's
Infinite fires.

Those who think that wealth
Can buy them love
Only play the fool
And meet with scorn.

‎כט‎ ‎8~‎

אָחוֹת לָנוּ קְטַנָּה
וְשָׁדַיִם אֵין לָהּ
מַה־נַּעֲשֶׂה לַאֲחֹתֵנוּ
בַּיּוֹם שֶׁיְּדֻבַּר־בָּהּ:

אִם־חוֹמָה הִיא
נִבְנֶה עָלֶיהָ טִירַת כָּסֶף
וְאִם־דֶּלֶת הִיא
נָצוּר עָלֶיהָ לוּחַ אָרֶז:

אֲנִי חוֹמָה
וְשָׁדַי כַּמִּגְדָּלוֹת
אָז הָיִיתִי בְעֵינָיו
כְּמוֹצְאֵת שָׁלוֹם:

ঌ 29

WE HAVE A YOUNG SISTER
WHOSE BREASTS ARE BUT FLOWERS.
WHAT SHALL WE DO
WHEN THE TIME COMES FOR SUITORS?

IF SHE'S A WALL
WE'LL BUILD TURRETS OF SILVER,
BUT IF SHE'S A DOOR
WE WILL PLANK HER WITH CEDAR.

I am a wall
And my breasts are towers!
So I have found peace
Here with my lover.

ל ‌8

כֶּרֶם הָיָה לִשְׁלֹמֹה
בְּבַעַל הָמוֹן
נָתַן אֶת־הַכֶּרֶם לַנֹּטְרִים
אִישׁ יָבִא בְּפִרְיוֹ
אֶלֶף כָּסֶף:

כַּרְמִי שֶׁלִּי לְפָנָי
הָאֶלֶף לְךָ שְׁלֹמֹה
וּמָאתַיִם לְנֹטְרִים אֶת־פִּרְיוֹ:

ও৺ 30

The king has a vineyard
Whose fruit is worth silver.
I have a vineyard—
Its fruit is my own.

Have your wealth, Solomon!
Keep all your vineyards,
Whose yield you must share
With your watchmen and guards.

✥ לא

הַיּוֹשֶׁבֶת בַּגַּנִּים
חֲבֵרִים מַקְשִׁיבִים לְקוֹלֵךְ
הַשְׁמִיעִינִי:

בְּרַח ׀ דוֹדִי
וּדְמֵה־לְךָ לִצְבִי
אוֹ לְעֹפֶר הָאַיָּלִים
עַל הָרֵי בְשָׂמִים:

ᐖ 31

Woman
of the gardens,
of the voice
friends listen for,
will you let me hear you?

Go—
go now, my love,
be quick
as a gazelle
on the fragrant hills!

הֵנֵצוּ הָרִמּוֹנִים

ða

And the pomegranate boughs unfold their blossoms

TRANSLATOR'S
STUDY

CHAPTER I

Translation
as a Journey

All journeys have secret destinations of which the traveler is unaware.

—Martin Buber[1]

ALL TRANSLATIONS necessarily imply departures from what might be posited as literal readings. I say "what might be posited" because the literal level is a hypothetical concept; although we speak of some translations as being more literal than others, there can be no *truly* literal translation of a literary text.[2] It is often impossible to find an equivalent for even a single word; how can one hope to translate a string of words without altering some element of syntax, or semantics, or sound? Indeed, the translator faces choices—often very close ones—at every step along the way.

Choosing one word over others, one inevitably sacrifices overtones and connotations; thus we often speak of things "lost in translation." Yet there are also gains. Translation is a kind of journey, a "carrying across" from one cultural-linguistic context to another. While experienced travelers know to shed baggage that becomes unnecessary along the way, they may also find themselves unexpectedly acquiring new possessions. So too, when texts are carried from one language to another, the losses and gains are often unpredictable. Translating entails risks—with departure as the first step in a largely unforeseeable sequence of movements.

Having departed from a text by deciding to translate it, by envisioning its shape and sound in a language not its own, the translator's next gesture is toward the text again—into its details and subtleties, its flaws, peculiarities, and perfections. The enveloping mists are lifted and the landscape eyed up close; one must see the smallest rocks and narrowest ravines, as well as the sweeping contours of the mountains. But then, once intimacy is established, the translator must leave again, taking another step away from the text to begin the utterance that will be the new work. For the translation too must have a life of its own, one that breathes to its own rhythms; it cannot exist without its own nourishing atmosphere. Thus the process of translation is a to-and-fro voyage, toward and away from the shores of the text, until finally one disembarks on new land.[3]

Yet we speak of fidelity in translation; we assume this is the translator's aim. Fidelity suggests attachment and commitment. How is such loyalty reconciled with all the leave-taking a translator must do?

There is no contradiction here. Fidelity means being close, not clinging to surfaces. It means fulfilling a trust, an obligation to be true to the relationship between self and other. A faithful translation of a text accurately represents its best and fullest appreciation by a reader. If that reader is sensitive, the appreciation will not be idiosyncratic, but it necessarily will be subjective. There is no way around it: translation emerges from interpretation, a "going between" self and other that can never be wholly objective but that strives for truth all the same.

Thus, each translator explores the relationship between text and reader in order to speak it anew, and each relationship has its own emphasis. Some translators, for example, concentrate on semantic accuracy, while others seek to re-create tone and mood. Most translators strive for a balance among the many facets of a text, but each balance is unique; there is no formula for faithful translation.

The concept of fidelity is even more complex with poetic texts, for with poetry the choices between form and content tend to be more subtle and more conflictual. Suppose for a moment that one wanted to translate into English a classical Chinese poem written in strict poetic form that included rhyme, syllable count, and parallelism. One might choose to sacrifice strictness of form in order to translate the poem's content faithfully; conversely, since the form is so integral to the original, one might prefer to preserve it at the expense of some element of content, such as imagery. Suppose one made the latter choice: *what* form would one then use—that of the original Chinese verse, or something more amenable to English, like the form of the Shakespearean sonnet? Attempting to reproduce Chinese poetic form in the English language would likely result in awkwardness rather than grace; thus one might choose the sonnet, which could be seen as analogous to (rather than a reproduction of) the form of the original. But then again, one might argue that a T'ang-dynasty poem is *by definition* formal, whereas a modern English poem certainly is not, and that therefore the effects of a sonnet's rhyme and meter in a modern English version would be wholly different from the effects of rhyme, syllable count, and parallelism in the original classical Chinese verse. Having come full circle, one might end up translating the poem in open form (free verse) after all. Thus, the arguments about what constitutes faithful translation of poetry can and do go on without limit or resolution, for they have to do with how we understand the very nature of poetry.

Perhaps no factor is more challenging to the translator than great historical distance, for what we think we understand of ancient texts often proves insufficient when we try to translate. With limited knowledge of the cultural context of a work, one may find it difficult to imagine original effects or guess at literary intentions. And when there is nowhere to turn for the very meanings of words that have gone out of use, the translator's task can indeed be frustrating.

The translator can, however, turn this disadvantage into a challenge. For now the need for personal involvement is intensified, and there is no choice but to engage the self entirely with the textual object. The results of this engagement are conclusions or, more precisely, postulations about what the text may have meant, how it may have been perceived in its own time. Thus, faithful translation, like original linguistic creativity, is a deeply subjective human enterprise. The relationship between translator and text is analogous to that between writer and subject matter: the same intense bearing of the self upon perception of the other is necessary to make a work of art happen.

My translation of the Song of Songs, a poetic text more than two millennia old, composed in a language for which there are no native speakers today,[4] is the result of an extended personal engagement. The process began with listening, moved to study and research, then led me to speculations and, finally, interpretations. These interpretations were the seeds I then took with me to plant in the terrain of my native language.

&

But why did I embark on such a venture? Why a new translation of the Song? Why not stop with the King James Version or the scores of English versions that have followed it?

The answer is that, although the King James is a classic, there *is* a need for a new translation, which has not been filled. From the perspective of scholarship alone, much has been learned since the time of the King James Version that makes apparent its many inaccuracies of meaning. In addition, modern analysis reveals that the King James Version, despite its eloquence, did biblical verse a disservice by treating it no differently from biblical prose. We cannot discern, from the King James Version, anything of the Song's internal literary structure, such as the poetic units it comprises. Nor do we sense from it the Hebrew poetic line: the long, cadenced lines of the King James Version correspond not to the actual breath/syntax units of the Hebrew, but to the demarcated "verses" (*pᵉsuqim*). Probably because of this, English readers tend to think of biblical poetry as extenuated and oracular—like that of Christopher Smart or Walt Whitman. Nothing could be less true. The Hebrew lines are relatively short units, of two, three, or four beats, with anywhere from two to five such lines making up the average biblical verse. (The next chapter, which treats the literary structure of the Song, explains further the distinction between poetic lines and *pᵉsuqim,* and also takes up the question of how one delineates the original poems in the Hebrew.)

Despite modern scholarship and analysis, however, the standard modern English versions of the Bible have not offered satisfying alternatives to the King James. The Revised Standard Version of 1952, for example, which is "an authorized revision of the American Standard Version, published in 1901, which was a revision of the King James Version," endeavors to correct the errors of its predecessors and to preserve "those qualities which have given to the King James Version a supreme place in English literature."[5] Yet, as literature, the Revised Standard Version has been far less influential than the King James. This is because, like many twentieth-century Bible translations, the Revised Standard Version speaks not in an authentic modern English voice but in a stilted echo of archaic rhythms and diction. The language does not reveal itself as true to either the speech or the literature of its day despite—or perhaps because of—the authors' attempt to preserve the literary qualities of the King James. Other, more recent, modern versions try consciously to offer language that is more accessible to modern readers; yet rarely do these versions achieve an idiom that is at once accessible *and moving*. Some of these attempt to render the Song as poetry by giving it the overt semblance of a literary structure; they do this by such means as dividing the text into sections (sometimes labeled as "poems") and identifying personae in the margins. The inclusion of headings and marginalia, however, does not suffice to turn a work into poetry. Indeed, none of the modern Bible versions offers a fully realized rendition of the Song as a poetic genre written in genuine poetic lines.

Translation as a Journey

The authors of the King James Version, by contrast, were neither imitating nor updating, but creating; their translation partook of the best literary style of its time. This made it moving and authentic, a work of integrity. And in this sense the King James Version was more faithful to the original than were the modern versions that followed it, because, in its own context, it had both accessibility and depth—qualities that the Hebrew text must have had in its original milieu. In other words, the King James Version, unlike its successors, reads not like a translation but like literature.

What is needed today, then, is a modern English translation of the Song that incorporates the insights of new scholarship and analysis yet reads like genuine poetry. I have attempted to fill that need.

≈

A brief look here at another modern Bible translation, one quite different from my own, may help to clarify some of the points I wish to make concerning my methods and goals. The German translation of Martin Buber and Franz Rosenzweig, begun in 1925 and completed by Buber in 1961, is, though not well known to English readers, a unique and monumental work. It raises issues not addressed by other versions of the Bible; indeed, it may represent the boldest challenge to Bible translation in the twentieth century.[6]

Buber's and Rosenzweig's primary aim was to revive the spoken quality of the Hebrew text for a contemporary German audience. To do this, they took considerable license with the German language, deliberately wrenching it from its own natural rhythms in an attempt to startle, and thus awaken, the ear of the German hearer. Buber stated his intention as follows: "German spoken forms can never reproduce the Hebrew spoken forms, but, growing out of analogous impulses and exerting analogous effects, they can correspond to them in German, render them into German."[7] In other words, the main principle behind their translation was "not to Germanize the Hebrew but to Hebraize the German."[8]

While Buber and Rosenzweig began with an appreciation of the text as spoken, they ended up with a German version that was, to a great extent, unspeakable: it was nothing like the normal spoken German of its time. As the eminent scholar of Jewish philosophy Gershom Scholem put it, in a lecture given at an occasion marking the completion of the translation, "The language into which you translated was not that of everyday speech nor that of German literature in the 1920's."[9] Unfortunately, the Buber-Rosenzweig translation never had a chance to test itself with German speakers because the audience for whom it was intended, the German-Jewish population, was all but totally extinguished in the Holocaust. Still, the Buber-Rosenzweig approach is not dead: it has been taken up again today by the American Bible translator Everett Fox, in his ongoing translation of the Torah.[10]

My own translation does not follow in this tradition, despite the fact that I, like Fox, began with some of the same assumptions that Buber and Rosenzweig held. I share their conviction that the text's original *spoken* quality supersedes in importance its nature as a written document (the common Hebrew word for Bible, *miqra'*, means not "scripture," but "calling out"). And I believe, as Buber and Rosenzweig did, that translations, like original texts, should be read aloud. Unlike Buber and Rosenzweig, however, I do not believe that Bible translations ought somehow to sound like the original. Rather, I think translations are more likely to be spoken aloud when they are written unselfconsciously, in the natural rhythms of their own languages.

Scholem remarked to Buber in his speech, "It is a unique feature of your translation that it uses every means to force the reader to read the text aloud." But one wonders *which* text the reader will be coerced into declaiming—the translation or the original? Perhaps the most revealing remark in Scholem's lecture is that the Buber-Rosenzweig translation "was an appeal to the reader: Go and learn Hebrew!" I think it is this that comes closest to the truth; the Buber-Rosenzweig translation does not, finally, stand on its own as German literature but performs instead a very different service. By approximating the rhythmic patterns of the Hebrew language, it seeks to engage the curiosity of readers who do not know Hebrew, enough perhaps to make them want to experience the sound of the original. Precisely by failing to satisfy the German literary sensibility, it whets the reader's appetite to learn Hebrew. It is, in this sense, a noble enterprise whose ultimate purpose is to make itself unnecessary.

My translation has no such aims. My goal is not to return the reader to the original, but to open the text as much as possible for English readers who cannot make Hebrew their own.

I do not attempt, in the lines of my renditions, to mimic the rhythms of Hebrew verse. English, an analytic language, requires more words to express thought than does the synthetic language of the Bible, which can, for example, incorporate subject, verb, and accusative pronoun into a single word. Thus English, unlike Hebrew, cannot easily articulate extended thoughts in lines of two or three beats. Yet to imitate the long-lined style of the King James would, as I have tried to show, reinforce misconceptions about biblical verse. My lines of verse are therefore a deliberate departure from the styles of both the King James Version and the original Hebrew text; they are of varying lengths, shaped by the demands of English poetic craft.

Indeed, a glance at the thirty-one poems in my version reveals a variety of verse forms: some poems are in couplets with off-rhymes, some are in iambic quatrains, some have accentual meter, some are in free verse, and so on. This variety is intended to reflect my view of the text as a collection of individual poems with a wide range of tones and moods. At the same time, I saw certain poems as related, sharing similar speakers, themes, or other features, and I tried to echo these continuities through the repetition of forms. Thus, for example, poems 8, 13, and 25—each spoken by a woman in the mode of fantasy and concluding with an adjuration refrain—are all rendered in accentual couplets.

To achieve the flexibility I needed in my craft, I steeped myself in the work of English and American writers, from the sixteenth- and seventeenth-century poets of England, artisans of meter and rhyme, to modern and contemporary American poets, innovators of open forms. To all these writers I owe the debt of tradition.

Above all, I owe these translations to their source, the place where the journey began.

CHAPTER 2

The Literary Structure
of the Song of Songs

PROBABLY NO BOOK in the Hebrew Bible has been the subject of more controversy concerning its classification as a genre than the Song of Songs. I do not intend to treat in any depth the long history of interpretation of the Song. H. H. Rowley has barely summarized the issue in forty-nine heavily footnoted pages,[1] and more recently Marvin Pope has taken up the matter in the lengthy introduction to his translation for the Anchor Bible series.[2] Pope covers every aspect of the history of the Song's interpretation, from the earliest Jewish and Christian allegorizations to contemporary feminist perspectives, including along the way psychoanalytic, melodramatic, cultic, and mystical approaches.[3] These theories, however, do not bear equally on literary questions, which are the chief concern of this study. For example, some interpretations emphasize original life setting (*Sitz im Leben*), while others are primarily interested in the religious significance of the text. In this chapter I will consider the major positions only as they are relevant to the literary structure of the Song; then I will explain my own reconstruction of the text as a collection of thirty-one poems.

The Literary Structure of the Song of Songs

The major interpretations view the Song as:

(a) an allegory of love between God and the people of Israel (the Jewish allegorical interpretation), or between Christ and the church or the individual soul (the Christian allegorical interpretation);

(b) a drama having two main characters, Solomon and the Shulammite, or three main characters, Solomon and two country lovers;

(c) a cycle of wedding songs, similar to Syrian marriage songs;

(d) a liturgy, the residue of an ancient fertility cult;

(e) a structurally unified love poem;

(f) a collection or anthology of love poems.

Of these interpretations, the allegorical—whose long history originated in the early Rabbinic period, first century C.E.—usually implies narrative structure, at least to the extent that it assumes plot development and posits fixed personae for the Song's voices. But neither plot nor fixed personae are obvious in the text, which does not name any of its speakers. (Solomon is not one of the Song's speakers; the mention of his name in the title and elsewhere will be discussed in subsequent chapters.) As we shall see in the next chapter, many different voices are heard in the Song, not just the two or three main characters implied by allegorical interpretation. Moreover—perhaps most significantly—the Song contains no mention of the name of God. Unlike, for example, Isaiah 5, the "parable of the vineyard," the Song itself never claims to be an allegory and nowhere offers an internal key to allegorical explication. It is likely that the allegorical interpretation arose in early Rabbinic times as a means of justifying the Song's place in the biblical canon; despite its imaginative richness, this interpretation carries no credence today outside the religious world.

The dramatic view of the Song—which dates back to Origen in the third century C.E. and gained currency in the nineteenth century, particularly among French and German scholars—also must be rejected on structural grounds. I know of no dramatic interpretation that has not distorted the Song considerably, usually by assuming a dramatis personae and scenarios not provided in the text itself, and sometimes by rearranging lines or whole passages.[4] The Song as we have it simply does not conform to dramatic structure, despite the fact that it comprises monologues and dialogues and seems to have a chorus that interjects from time to time. The presence of monologues, dialogues, and choruses is insufficient basis on which to posit drama, because drama, like narrative, implies plot and the unified portrayal of characters.

The view of the Song as a cycle of wedding poems—a theory that arose in the nineteenth century—does not assume plot but does assume a fixed set of speakers (bride, groom, and guests) in the context of a marriage celebration. The twentieth-century theory holding that the Song is the liturgy of an ancient fertility cult also suggests fixed personae in a fixed content. The latter view may be seen, ironically, as a return to religious interpretation of the Song; in recent times it has attracted particular attention among those interested in ancient goddess worship. Both views of the

Song—as wedding poems and as liturgy—are based on rather elaborate postulations about the text's original life setting and its relationship to other ancient Near Eastern cultures. While they may account for some of the material in the Song, or at least for some of its influences, these theories do not explain the Song as a whole. Rather, they impose awkward superstructures that are finally no more convincing than the allegorical or dramatic overviews. Moreover, they deny the obvious content of the Song, which is primarily concerned not with marriage or religious ritual but with the various emotions of erotic love.

The main objection to the four overviews outlined so far is their imposition of fixed personae and either plot or contextual unity on a text that seems instead to present a variety of voices speaking in a range of settings and without narrative sequence. Thus the supposition of allegory, drama, wedding celebration, or liturgy unnaturally constricts the variegated material of the Song. Recently, however, there have been attempts to demonstrate structural unity in the Song without presupposing such restrictive frameworks; these analyses read the Song as a unified love poem—the fifth overview mentioned above. Although each of these readings finds a different internal structure, J. Cheryl Exum's "A Literary and Structural Analysis of the Song of Songs"[5] serves as a good exemplar of the overall position. By briefly examining its argument, I hope to begin to make clear my own reasons for viewing the Song not as a unity but as a collection—the sixth position listed above.

Exum, who states her purpose to be a "formal analysis," treats the Song as three pairs of poems (2:7–3:5 and 5:2–6:3; 3:6–5:1 and 6:4–8:3; 1:2–2:6 and 8:4–14), examining the parallels among them. She proposes that the discovery of structural parallels yields the following conclusions: "Unity of authorship with an intentional design, and a sophistication of poetic style." Interestingly, Exum does not *argue* for "unity of authorship" except insofar as she demonstrates the unity of the text. Her deduction of "either a single author or a school of poets working closely together" perhaps seems obvious to her, given her demonstration of structural unity in the text, but one should also allow for the possibility that this unity was imposed by a later compiler.

With Exum's second conclusion, "sophistication of poetic style," I am quite in agreement. Indeed, one might question why she links this to her first conclusion, "unity of authorship with an intentional design," when the one is not dependent on the other. I see no reason to doubt that folk poetry—that is, the collective work of many authors—can be as sophisticated as the product of an individual author's hand. In any case, let us look at Exum's argument for *textual* unity, and treat the issue of authorship as derivative.

Exum claims that her division of the text into three parallel pairs of poems accounts for various repeated words and phrases, including refrains and recurrent motifs, such as "seeking and finding." But structural parallels are not necessary to account for the presence of these repetitions, which can be equally well explained by viewing the text as a collection of separate poems derived from a common cultural source. That is, the Song's repeated images may well have been literary conventions, much as Petrarchan imagery was conventional to Renaissance poetry.

Exum does more than note the mere presence of repeated material in the Song, however; she argues for "intentional design," or the specific *arrangement* of recurrent phrases and motifs. In so doing, she shows some interesting parallels among the poetic units *as she divides them*. Explaining her method, she says: "The criteria used to determine the limits of poems are the repetition of key phrases, words, and motifs, and the contextual coherence of the poems. Sometimes the limits of a poem are not apparent and we must rely on its parallel as a guide." While her method here may sometimes seem circular, the more serious limitation is that, in her effort to delineate parallels, Exum tends to overlook literary features that do not support her analysis. Attempting to demonstrate contextual coherence, she ignores many shifts in setting, argument, tone of voice, and speaker-audience relationship, which, I believe, strongly suggest smaller compositional units. As for the "key phrases, words, and motifs" that guide her delineations, these may in fact be evidence that the Song was orally composed and transmitted before being compiled and transcribed.[6] As Franz Landsberger explains, "We may assume that a compiler who puts into one collection poems which had hitherto circulated by way of mouth, would write them down according to the principle of association. Writing down one poem he would remember and write down another with a similar key word."[7]

The Literary
Structure
of the
Song of Songs

Thus, as suggested above, the "design" of the Song that Exum perceives—like that found by other proponents of her position—may well be the result of skillful compilation of many short poems rather than original structural unity. Or it may be the result of an ingenious interpretive reading that discerns pattern where none was originally conceived. It seems, in any case, that the search for structural unity, as pursued by Exum and others, necessitates a less attentive reading of the more subtle variations that appear in the text—and this is its gravest flaw. As I see it—and as I shall try to demonstrate in subsequent chapters—the Song opens up most fully to interpretation when it is viewed as a collection of many short lyrics.

Before presenting this final view of the Song and explaining my own reconstruction of it, I want to clarify one important reason for the endless and seemingly unresolvable debates over its structure. In the Leningrad MS., 1008 C.E. (one of the earliest complete manuscripts, today considered authoritative) of the Masoretic text of the Hebrew Bible (the standardized text, edited by fifth- to ninth-century scholars known as the Masoretes, or "transmitters"), we find the Song divided into chapters and smaller portions designed for reading in synagogues. Also indicated are *p'suqim,* units roughly equivalent to sentences but not necessarily poetic lines; these are what are called biblical "verses" in English. The Masoretic accent marks indicate caesuras within the *p'suqim* as well as conjunctive and disjunctive connections between words; otherwise there is nothing that might be considered punctuation. Poetic units are not apparent: no demarcation is given for individual poems, stanzas, or lines of verse. In other words, the text looks like a mass of prose on the page, divided only into

The Literary
Structure
of the
Song of Songs

sections and subsections of approximately equal length. Theoretically, then, the Song might be *seen* as having no poetic structure at all; hence the wide speculation surrounding it.

Yet hardly anyone would disagree that the Song *is* poetry, not prose.[8] This is because of its *audibly* apparent rhythms—that is, the heavy coincidence of syntactic/semantic units with units of accent or breath—and its unique style, which includes such elements as sound-plays, puns, and alliterations; an abundance of sensual imagery appealing to all the senses; a sophisticated and often subtle use of metaphor; and a flexible deployment of the biblical stylistic technique of parallelism. This rich combination of features creates a particularly heightened and intense language, which can lead one to view the Song not just as poetry but as the quintessential poetry of the Bible.

Now, a *minimal* definition of poetry or verse (at least in postbiblical Western tradition) might be that it is language in lines. In written verse, lines take a visual shape on the page, with stanza breaks usually indicating longer pauses. Line breaks and stanza breaks in written verse are, in effect, visual indications of how a poem is to be heard. Yet in the case of the Song the matter is reversed: because line and stanza divisions are not indicated, we must postulate, on the basis of what we can hear from reading the text aloud, where such divisions might have appeared had the text been transcribed as it was heard in its own time.

While there is no definitive theory of Hebrew prosody, scholars today agree in general about the identification of poetic lines of the text. This is because the Hebrew lines articulate themselves perceptibly in short units of breath having two, three, four, or, very rarely, five beats; these units generally coincide with syntactic units such as phrases or clauses (enjambement is rare). Thus the division into lines was for me the first and least problematic step in the reconstruction of the text as a poetic document.

Stanza breaks, a matter of less importance and more speculation, came much later in my reconstruction. In essence, my stanza divisions offer suggestions for reading the text aloud and a guide to hearing its meaning, but they are *not* meant to represent the way the original might have been transcribed in its own time, for it is not certain that the concept of stanzas applied to ancient Hebrew verse. Stanza breaks in my translation usually indicate one or more of the following: a change of speaker within a poem, a change of audience, a pause to allow time to pass in a narrative sequence, a pause to allow for closure and reopening of an extended theme. Sometimes the stanza divisions set off discrete metaphorical units, as in the *wasfs* (see chapter 4).

My division of the text into poems—unlike the division of poems into stanzas—*is* an attempt to postulate the Song's original structure. The presentation of the Song in the Leningrad MS. demonstrates why it may well be a collection rather than a unified poem. For if we assume (as virtually everyone does) line units where they are not visually indicated, there is no reason to exclude the possibility of poem units. The view of the text as a collection of several poems is shared by many—if not most—scholars.[9] Robert Gordis, in the introduction to his translation, traces this view back five centuries: "If the Song of Songs be approached without any preconception, it reveals itself as a collection of lyrics. This view of the book was taken by a Middle High German version of the 15th century, which divided it into 54 songs."[10]

The reasons for viewing the Song as a collection are many. Gordis notes "the wide gamut of its emotions"; we might add to this the several distinct settings, the range of situations and subject matter, and the considerable variety of tones and moods. By far the strongest argument, I believe, is the presence in the Song of many different speakers, addressing a variety of audiences. (In the next chapter I analyze the various relationships between speakers and audiences in the Song and attempt to demonstrate, on the basis of this analysis, the presence of several types of lyric poems in the collection.)

Of the interpreters who view the text as a collection and divide it as such, however, no two agree exactly on the divisions. Gordis finds twenty-eight poems in the Song, but notes other scholars who find, variously, twenty-three, twenty-six, eighteen, and so forth. Gordis also allows that, in his presentation, several of the poems are fragmentary and some may be "doublets." The fact that scholars differ in their division of the text does not undermine the belief that the Song is not a unity. As Gordis explains:

> The division of the songs will depend upon the changes
> in theme, viewpoint, background or form. These criteria
> will not always be sufficiently exact to command universal
> assent. Much will be dependent upon the literary taste
> and insight, as well as upon the knowledge, of the inter-
> preter. But this is simply a restatement of the truth that
> exegesis is essentially an art, which rests upon a founda-
> tion of scientific knowledge.

For my own division of the text into thirty-one poems, the perception of content guided the delineation of form. Besides the various shifts (of speaker, audience, subject matter, setting, tone) that signaled to me the end of one poem and the beginning of the next, the presence of self-contained arguments also suggested limits. For the most part, I found that individual poems had internal coherence and were not mere fragments.

For example, 1:2–4 of the Hebrew is a passage praising the beloved and inviting lovemaking, spoken by a woman to a man whom she compares to a king. The unit seems to close naturally with the refrain "they love you." The next line in the Hebrew brings us into a new context. A woman speaks, but her audience is the city women and her tone of voice is defiant. This passage, 1:5–6, is a monologue of self-assertion rather than of praise for the beloved; it does not appear to be a continuation of the previous speech. On the basis of these observations, I treat 1:2–4 and 1:5–6 as two separate poems.

There are, of course, instances where the divisions between poems are not so apparent. For example, poems 16 and 17 (of my reconstruction) are both invitations spoken by a man to his beloved, whom he calls "bride"; also, in both poems Lebanon is mentioned. One might therefore see the two as a single poem, but I saw sufficient reason to separate them. Whereas in poem 16 Lebanon is a dangerous place, the habitat of wild animals, in 17 it is associated with pleasant fragrance, like that of the beloved's clothing. The tone of 17 is gentler than that of 16 because its context is less threatening. The appearance of the words "bride" and "Lebanon" in both poems may be the result of an editorial juxtaposition; in other words, they may be the catchwords that led a compiler to place the poems alongside one another.[11] Finally, each poem makes a complete and separate argument: in 16, the woman is urged to leave her dangerous abode and join her lover; in 17, the speaker describes, from near rather than afar, the power of his beloved to excite him with her beauty and sensuality. Thus, while it is conceivable that the two poems were one, it benefits each to be read and heard separately.

We have seen how, in oral literature like the Song, content may suggest ways to delineate structure when structure is otherwise ambiguous. So too our perception of structure in the Song influences how we read its content. In the next chapter I explore the internal structure of the Song—the types of poems it comprises—as groundwork for further inquiry into its meaning.

CHAPTER 3

Types of Love Lyrics
in the Song of Songs

IF THE SONG OF SONGS is not a structural unity, what kind of compilation is it? I believe it is best described as a collection of lyrics, specifically, lyric love poems. The reader may not be satisfied with this definition, however, since the term "lyric," at least in common usage, tends to be somewhat impressionistic. I propose in this chapter to explore what we mean by this term—including obvious and less apparent meanings—and see how it applies to different types of poems in the Song.

Types of Love Lyrics in the Song of Songs

Let us begin with the obvious. If lyric verse is distinguished from narrative and dramatic verse primarily by length and scope, all the poems in the Song would have to be seen as lyrics. So too, if we think of the lyric as sensual, the exquisitely rich imagery of the Song would certainly qualify the Song as lyric poetry (more on the subject of sensuality and the senses in chapter 5).

Indeed, the Song fits the etymological definition, which proclaims the lyric to be musical or songlike. A lyric (from the Greek *lyra*, meaning "lyre") was originally a poem sung to musical accompaniment, and probably no other ancient text, at least in Western civilization, has been more often or more variously chanted, sung, and set to music. In this regard, the very title of the book—*šir hašširim*, "the Song of Songs"—is revealing. The relationship between poetry and song was undoubtedly a close one for the ancient Hebrews and is very likely related to the oral tradition from which the Song of Songs derives. Even beyond the time of its composition and compilation, the Song was orally transmitted by the Jews, who continue to this day to chant it ritually on the Sabbath of Passover. In communities that follow kabbalistic practice (such as those of the Yemenite Jews and of the Sephardic-Jewish descendants of Spain), the Song is chanted weekly, just prior to the onset of the Sabbath. The Masoretic accent marks, used as notation for cantillation, have provided the basis of long and continuous traditions, many of which are still alive today.

In addition to being ritually chanted, the words of the Song have often been set to music, a practice that has survived into the modern era. Indeed, in Israel today, composers and musicians continue to set the Song to new melodies, reconfirming its place in Hebrew oral culture. One may say without exaggeration that, if "lyric" means "songlike," the Song of Songs is a quintessentially lyric collection.

Brevity, sensuality, and musicality, however, do not suffice to characterize the lyric. The lyric, as we know it in the history of Western literature, tends to be a subjective form, expressive of personal feeling toward specific subject matter and addressed to a particular listener. The speaker of the lyric is usually a first-person singular voice, or I-speaker, although, as we shall see shortly, more than one voice may speak a lyric. While the subject matter of the lyric can vary widely—it may be simple or complex, commonplace or extraordinary, secular or religious, public or private—the speaker's relationship to that subject is almost always personal and intense. As for the audience of the lyric—by which I mean the listener whom the speaker addresses, not necessarily the readership of the poem—it too varies: it may be a beloved, a friend, a relation, a stranger, God, or even the self. The more intimate the relationship between speaker and audience, however, the more lyrical is the speech.

To see what kinds of lyrics the Song comprises, then, it may be useful to examine its speakers in relation to their subject matter and audience. In doing so, we may find Martin Buber's concept of *I-Thou* relation to be helpful. By *I-Thou* Buber refers to primary, mutual relationship, which he distinguishes from *I-It*, or subject-object experience.[1] In the various poems of the Song in which a lover speaks to or about a beloved,[2] we might say that the potential for *I-Thou* relation exists. This is perhaps most evident when a speaker directly addresses a beloved, but it may also be felt when the beloved is spoken of only in the third person. In other poems of the Song, however—those that have erotic subject matter but do not focus on the beloved or the personal love experience—the *I-Thou* quality may be subordinate or absent. The degree to which *I-Thou* relation is present in a poem provides one standard by which we may measure the poem's lyricism; thus, we shall keep this feature in view as we analyze the various types of poems in the Song.

Before proceeding, I want to define two terms: "monologue" and "dialogue." For the purposes of this discussion, a monologue is a poem having within it no change of speaker, whether that poem is spoken by an individual or by a group; a dialogue is a poem in which conversation takes place between speakers or groups of speakers. I do not imply by these terms any association with the genre of drama.

The following, then, are six types of lyrics that can be distinguished in the Song:

(a) the "love monologue"—a poem spoken by an I-speaker to and/or about a beloved, in which the beloved is the implicit, but not necessarily the explicit, audience (poems 1, 4, 5, 8, 10, 12, 13, 15, 16, 17, 20, 21 [symbolic], 23, 24, 25, 27, and 28);

(b) the "love dialogue"—a conversation between two lovers (poems 3, 6, 7, 9, 18, and 31);

(c) a monologue spoken by an I-speaker in a love relationship, to an audience outside that relationship (poems 2 and 30);

(d) a monologue spoken by an unidentifiable speaker (probably a group) to an unspecified audience, about erotic subject matter, either direct or symbolic (poems 11, 14, and 26);

(e) a dialogue between an I-speaker and a group of speakers, about erotic subject matter (poems 22 and 29);

(f) the composite poem—a love monologue within which other speech, including both monologues and dialogues, is recorded (poem 19).

(a) Love monologues—poems in which a single speaker, female or male, speaks to or about a beloved—make up over half the poems in the Song. Often in the love monologues, the beloved is directly addressed, and therefore is the *explicit* audience of the speech. Even when the beloved is not directly addressed, however, we might say that she or he, as the true focus of the speaker's feelings, remains the *implicit* audience. Thus, the love monologue sometimes has a double audience: an apparent (explicit) hearer, such as a group of people outside the love relationship, and the true (implicit) audience, who is always the beloved.

Double audiences are found more frequently in love monologues spoken by females than in those spoken by males. Of the love monologues spoken by a woman (poems 1, 5, 8, 12, 13, 24, 25, 27, and 28) all but 27 and 28 refer in part, if not entirely, to the beloved in the third person, thus implying some other audience besides him.[3] Often, as in all or parts of poems 5, 8, 12, 13, and 24, the speaker seems to be addressing herself—wishing, anticipating, or daydreaming—as in a fantasy. In poems 8, 13, and 25, she explicitly addresses another audience, the "women of the city." In all these poems, however, the focus of feeling remains the beloved; he is the implicit audience of all these speeches. In poem 13, the speaker cannot address her beloved explicitly because he is absent, but the longing she expresses can be satisfied only by him. In 8, the food she requests, ostensibly from the city women (the Hebrew imperatives are directed to a plural "you"), is a metaphor for erotic attention, which only the beloved can actually provide.

Thus *I-Thou* relation is strongly implied in all the love monologues spoken by women, even those ostensibly addressed to listeners other than the beloved. *I-Thou* relation may seem more obvious, however, in the love monologues spoken by men (poems 4, 10, 15, 16, 17, 20, 21, and 23) because all of these, with the exception of poem 21, *explicitly* address the beloved. The male speakers of love monologues, unlike the females, never address a specified group of outsiders such as the city women, and only twice—in poems 21 and 23—do they seem to address themselves. In poem 21, we cannot in fact be certain of the gender of the speaker or the audience (the Hebrew leaves the question open), but the content of the poem, viewed symbolically, provides some clues. The speaker walks through a garden ("orchard" in my translation), eyeing the pomegranates and vines. Elsewhere in the Song, the garden is associated with female sexuality, as are the images of vines and pomegranates (see the discussions of vines and gardens in "Six Central Motifs," chapter 5). This small spring song seems to be a self-addressed male fantasy—a veiled description of an anticipated union with the beloved. The mode of fantasy seems also to dominate poem 23, which is addressed partly to the beloved and partly to the self.[4]

Because male speakers in the love monologues (and, in fact, throughout the Song) only rarely seem to fantasize or address third persons but instead address their beloveds explicitly, one might conjecture that, in the Song's original culture (as in ours), males were allowed more forthrightness than females. But women's speech in the Song is hardly reserved or shy; on the contrary, it is uninhibited and even outspoken, and the Song's female speakers do not hesitate to initiate action. The propensity to fantasize thus does not seem to be inversely related to the ability to speak or act directly; at least among female speakers, both modes are prevalent, and one is not a substitute for the other.

Indeed, women may be seen as the Song's central figures primarily *because* of their full participation in both direct and indirect kinds of speech, including modes of self-address. As Shelomo Dov Goitein notes: "In the majority of verses it is a woman who speaks, who acts, and, most significantly, who reflects. The book is conveyed to us mostly from the meditation of a woman's heart and not a man's."[5] Chaim Rabin goes even further, proposing that the entire Song may be a woman's fantasy. He notes that the female speaker is the "chief person in the Song," and that "she expresses deep and complicated emotions" compared with those expressed by the male. Rabin continues: "It is surely significant that there are a number of occasions when he speaks in her imagination, but never she in his. . . . A case could be made out for the theory that everything the lover says is imagined by her, even if this is not expressly stated."[6]

Rabin's rather unusual proposal that we view the Song as entirely a female's fantasy (a proposal I do not finally accept) is perhaps not altogether surprising: one cannot help but be impressed both by the preponderance of female speech in the Song and by its variety, richness, and authenticity. Unlike most of the Bible, the Song of Songs gives us women speaking out of their own experiences and their own imaginations, in words that do not seem filtered through the lens of patriarchal male consciousness. As Carol Meyers writes: "The society depicted in the Bible is portrayed primarily from a male perspective, in terms of male accomplishments and in relation to a God for whom andromorphic imagery predominates. Yet in the Song, such characteristics disappear and in fact the opposite may be true; that is, a gynocentric mode predominates."[7] In the Song, that is to say, women are central, not peripheral, and, I would add, their speech seems "true," not imitative.

Yet, I would also add, this is not to posit female domination or to imply that men are derivative. The speech of men in the Song, even if limited to fewer modes (and somewhat fewer lines) than that of women, also seems true—that is, not filtered through women's imaginations, but authentically self-expressive. Indeed, I would argue that men's speech in the Song is *as* authentic as women's, despite—or actually, because of—the overwhelming linguistic similarity between the two. The equally rich, sensual, emotionally expressive, and often playful language of the Song's female and male voices (whether they are speaking directly or indirectly, to others or to themselves) seems to evidence a nonsexist, nonhierarchical culture—unique in the Bible. Rather than offering a reversal of stereotypical male-female relations, the Song provides a different model, one in which *all* hierarchical domination is absent. Thus the Song expresses mutuality and balance between the sexes, along with an absence of stereotyped notions of masculine and feminine behavior and characteristics.[8] (I will pursue the subject of mutuality further in the discussion of the love dialogues, next, and I will take up related issues concerning male and female representations in chapter 4.)

Finally, the love monologues of both women and men—which are always intense, personal, and aimed *ultimately* at an audience of one, the beloved *Thou*—seem to be the purest form of lyric expression in the Song.

(b) Love dialogues are poems in which two lovers speak to each other with invitations, mutual praise, or questions and replies. Because the two voices are I-speakers, each expressing personal feeling to and about the other, we may consider these dialogues variations of the love lyric, even though the lyric is usually thought of as the speech of a single voice. Poems 3, 6, 7, 9, 18, and 31 are all examples of this type, although poem 9 is, strictly, a monologue within a monologue. It is a woman's speech, in which the speaker records her lover's words; thus, she refers to him in the third person, but he addresses her in the second person. Poem 18 also departs slightly from the dialogue form, in that it concludes with the interjection of a third voice addressing the lovers.

While the love dialogues are often similar in tone, and all share the setting of the domesticated countryside, the most significant feature that they have in common is their expression of intimacy, or reciprocity of emotion. This reciprocity, characteristic of *I-Thou* relation, is obvious in the love dialogues because they are (with the exception of poem 9) direct conversations. Not only do two speakers express mutual feelings; they often use similar metaphors and sometimes identical phrases to describe their appreciation. For example, in poem 7, a man describes his beloved as a flower among brambles; she responds by describing him as a fruit tree in the thickets. In poem 6, a woman responds to her lover's exclamation, "How fine / you are, my love," with a similar outburst, "How fine / are you, my lover." In poem 3, a woman's request for information from her lover—"Tell me, my love, where you feed your sheep / And where you rest in the afternoon"—may seem to elicit an evasive response; but in fact the tone of *both* voices is coy. This dialogue appears to be a lovers' game of hide-and-seek. Similarly, the woman's reply to her lover in poem 31 may sound like a rejection—"go now"—but as we will see (chapter 5), it is actually a veiled invitation to return later.

Because the feeling of reciprocity is central to these dialogues, I have sometimes emphasized this prosodically in the translations. For example, the English poem 7 is in iambic quatrains, each closing with the word "love." This refrain, introduced to call attention to the parallel imagery of the two voices, substitutes for the synonymous parallelism—a prosodic technique of biblical verse—that characterizes these voices in the Hebrew and helps create the poem's strong feel-

Types of Love Lyrics in the Song of Songs

ing of mutuality. In the English of poem 31 a different technique is used to a similar purpose: here, each of the two voices speaks an equal number of lines, divided into parallel rhythmic units.

Because always two voices speak the love dialogues, these poems depart from a traditional conception of lyric form. But as love poems they express perhaps most perfectly the mutuality of *I-Thou* love in the Song's paradisiacally nonsexist world.

(c) Poems 2 and 30 are monologues spoken by an I-speaker, but not to a beloved, and only symbolically and secondarily about a beloved; in neither poem is the beloved felt to be the implicit audience. Although erotic relationships are alluded to in both poems (the vines and vineyards are sexual symbols), they are not the focus of the speeches. In poem 2, a woman addresses an audience of city women, that is, people outside any intimate love bond. Similarly in poem 30, a man addresses first an unspecified audience and then King Solomon, a figure of public power and wealth. The king is a foil for the speaker, whose defiant tone is similar to that of the speaker in poem 2. Both poems express self-pride more than love for an other, and although the self-esteem of the speakers is bolstered by erotic relationships in the background, the beloveds are not nearly as prominent as in the poems of types (a) and (b). The intensity of the speakers' personal feeling toward their subject matter in poems 2 and 30 contributes to the poems' lyricism, but these poems are far less expressive of *I-Thou* feeling than are the love monologues and love dialogues. I have rendered 2 and 30 in metrical quatrains for formal effect.

(d) Poems 11, 14, and 26 are monologues spoken by unidentifiable speakers to unspecified audiences (except for the last stanza of poem 14, which is explicitly addressed to the daughters of Jerusalem). These poems refer, either directly or symbolically (in poem 11, through the image of the vines), to erotic relationships, but they are spoken by outside observers rather than participants. While their mood is animated, it is doubtful whether *personal* feeling is expressed. Although we cannot be certain on the basis of content or grammar, the tone of these poems suggests groups of voices rather than individual speakers. In this way these poems are unlike the other monologues in the text and are less lyrical in expression. Because the personae of these poems are unclear, I set the English poems in the typeface designating unidentifiable speakers.

(e) The dialogue poems 22 and 29 differ from the love dialogues in that neither offers an *I-Thou* conversation; rather, each of these dialogues is between an individual and a group of speakers. Poem 22 is dominated by a group of voices, probably men's, praising a female dancer, who herself speaks but two lines. In tone and feeling, 22 most resembles poem 14 (of type d), where a chorus of voices (here probably women) describes the beauty of the marriage procession. In poem 29, a young sister replies to her protective older brothers with a tone of self-pride similar to that of the speakers of poems 2 and 30 (of type c). Although the subject matter of both 22 and 29 is erotic, *I-Thou* love is not the primary focus of either. I have rendered poems 22 and 29, as poems 14, 2, and 30, with metrical forms.

(f) The composite poem, 19, constituting about an eighth of the entire Song, includes the voices of several speakers, in monologues and dialogues, explicitly addressing several audiences. It is set in a variety of contexts, shifting from the bedroom to the city streets and concluding in the garden. It also spans a range of moods, and seems even to have dramatic development, including climax and denouement. But its frame—its opening and closing lines, which govern the poem's situation—is that of a love monologue spoken by an I-speaker whose beloved is, throughout, the implicit audience. Thus, despite its length and structural complexity, which suggests some narrative and dramatic features, it is essentially lyric in expression.

The poem begins with a woman's declaration that, even as she sleeps, her heart remains awake. It is thus the only self-proclaimed dream poem in the collection, although, as we have seen, the dreamlike modes of wishing, anticipating, and daydreaming appear in several other poems. Relating her dream to an unspecified audience, possibly herself, the

Types of Love Lyrics in the Song of Songs

speaker records the voice of her lover at the door. Thus far the poem is a monologue within a monologue, similar in structure to poem 9. But now the woman responds to her lover's invitation, explicitly addressing herself: "Should I get up, get dressed, / and dirty my feet?" After this, the narrative element takes over, as the speaker describes a sequence that takes her from her bed to the door and finally into the city streets in search of her beloved. At the onset of this narrative sequence, the distinction between dream and waking life becomes blurred; it is unclear whether subsequent events happen within the speaker's dream or whether she is now awake.

Recounted in the narration is a terrifying encounter with the city guards: "The men who roam the streets, / guarding the walls, / beat me and tear away my robe." Following this moment of violence, which is unmatched anywhere else in the Song, the speaker, now quite distraught, turns from her storytelling to appeal directly to the city women. She asks them for help in finding her beloved, and they answer, skeptically, with a question: who *is* your love, that you make this demand on us? The woman then responds with a lengthy description of her beloved in the form of a *wasf* (the features of the *wasf* are discussed in chapter 4). This *wasf* constitutes a love monologue, similar to the one spoken by a male in poem 15, although here the beloved is referred to throughout in the third person. The closing lines of the *wasf* affirm the mutuality of the *I-Thou* relationship and climax the poem.

The poem concludes with a short dialogue between the woman and the city women, who have been the explicit audience of this *wasf*. Impressed by her description of her beloved, they are now quite ready to help her find him; but she has apparently calmed herself with her own recollection of his beauty and no longer wants the help that they are so eager (perhaps overeager?) to give. She tells the city women that her beloved is in "his garden" (with her) and that the love relationship is intact. Thus, in the closing stanzas of the poem, the woman reaffirms the *I-Thou* relationship and excludes her explicit audience, the city women, from participation in it. The poem ends on a note of intimacy: anticipated reunion with the beloved.

The biggest challenge in translating this poem was finding a form that would hold together its various sections and at the same time reveal similarities between these sections and the other poems in the collection. After much experimentation, I settled on a combination of free verse and metrical forms. I began with lines of free verse to introduce the anxious dream-speech, then shifted to metrical lines for the dialogue with the city women. I rendered the *wasf* in iambic quatrains (similar to the treatment of the *wasf* in poem 22) and repeated the same meter in the concluding two stanzas, to extend the affirmative tone of the *wasf* into the poem's resolution. Thus, if the English translation of poem 19 looks like a small compilation of even smaller lyrics, it is because I wished to highlight its composite form.

੨੦

This analysis has attempted to reveal similarities and differences among poems in the Song based on the degrees to which they share various features of the lyric and on the ways in which they express romantic and erotic love. We have seen that all the poems treat aspects of love and eros, and that all may be classified as lyrics. But some poems—those in which an *I-Thou* relationship is central—seem to be *archetypal* love lyrics, whereas others may be seen as variations on this archetype. The collection as a whole emerges as a variegated compilation of several types of love lyrics, expressing a wide range of feeling and tone.

CHAPTER 4

The Waṣf

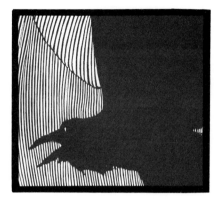

IT IS A PARADOX of human nature that strangeness, like its   *The Wasf*
opposite, often breeds contempt. While the Song has been
widely celebrated by Bible scholars and lay audiences alike,
there is another mood—of uneasiness, even embarrass-
ment—that sometimes murmurs beneath the din of the ap-
plause. This discontent seems to surface in scholarly
discussions of a kind of passage known as the *wasf;* these discussions not only reveal some of the limitations of Bible
scholarship in the realm of literary study, but they also ex-
pose some of the prejudices most frequently applied to the
Song as a whole. Primarily to shed light on these problems
and to suggest solutions—including a method of interpretation that I used while translating—I treat the *wasf* as a separate subject here.

Wasf, an Arabic word meaning "description," has come
to refer to a particular kind of poetic passage that describes
through a series of images the parts of the human body.
While *wasf*s are not uncommon in modern Arabic poetry, in
ancient Hebrew literature they appear only in the Song of
Songs. The similarity between certain passages in the Song
and modern Arabic poems was discovered in the last century; as a result, the technical term *wasf* has become familiar
in scholarly studies of the Song.

Although the *wasf* shares stylistic features with the rest
of the Song, relying for poetic effect on metaphor, imagery,
parallelisms, and sound-plays, it is formally stricter and more
predictable than any other material in the collection. Essentially a catalogue that describes in sequence (from top to bottom or bottom to top) segments of the male or female body,
the *wasf* appears, in whole or in part, in several different
types of poems in the Song. Poem 15 is a love monologue
containing a partial *wasf;* 19 is a composite containing a complete *wasf;* 20 is a love monologue that repeats part of the
wasf found in 15; and 22, framed as a dialogue, contains another complete *wasf.* Of these four *wasf*s, those in poems 15,
20, and 22 are descriptions of a female, while that in 19 describes a male.

Not only is the form of the *wasf* fairly rigid and its subject matter determined at the outset, but its treatment of the

The Wasf subject also follows a pattern: each part of the physique is described by means of specific, often unlikely images drawn from the realms of nature and artifice. While the imagery in the *wasf* is usually visual, sometimes it appeals to other senses, as in the tactile "breasts like fawns" or the aromatic "lips like lilies."

It has been my observation that the imagery in the *wasfs* is often associated by English readers with the "peculiar" poetic character of the Song and with the "exotic" nature of ancient Hebrew sensibility. When giving readings of my translation, I find audiences especially curious to hear how I rendered those strings of strange images known to them previously through the standard translations. More difficult to understand, however, is the reaction to the *wasf* of Bible scholars, who are presumably familiar enough with ancient Hebrew culture not to find it exotic. Here are some typical examples of what the scholars have to say:

> To our sensibilities the images are admittedly comical and puzzling. Consequently, one must infer either that this was the poet's intention, in which case the *wasfs* are not "descriptive love songs" at all but parodies, or that our perspective radically differs from the poet's.[1]

> Only as playful banter can be rationally explained the grotesque description by the lover to the damsel of her neck as "like the tower of David built for an armoury," of her nose "as the tower of Lebanon which looketh toward Damascus," and of her head like mount Carmel (iv 4, vii 5, 6), and similar comical comparisons of her other limbs.[2]

> The comparison of the girl's hair to a flock of goats would have been straightforward and legitimate if mention of the slopes of Gilead had been omitted. As the image stands, the mountain background is, in reference to a girl's head, too large for the goats, for if they are bunched together there are too many slopes bare of goats, but if they are scattered the emphasis falls upon the girl's hairs rather than her hair. Thus the figure is bizarre, if not grotesque, possibly by intent of the author.[3]

"Comical," "puzzling," "bizarre," "grotesque"—do these words aptly describe the imagery in the Song? If so, what words might describe acclaimed passages in English literature, such as the conceits of the metaphysical poets: for

example, Crashaw's comparison in "The Weeper" of Mary   *The Wasf*
Magdalene's tears to "two faithful fountains; / Two walking
baths; two weeping motions; / Portable, and compendious
oceans"; or Donne's two lovers like legs of a compass in "A
Valediction: Forbidding Mourning"? And how shall we
characterize the poetry of the modern age, including the im-
agism of writers like Pound, Moore, Williams, H. D.? Will
it not seem odd to find poets comparing the view inside a
subway station to a branch of a tree, as in Pound's famous
two-line poem "In a Station of the Metro": "The apparition
of these faces in the crowd; / Petals on a wet, black bough"?
How will we even begin to understand foreign literatures
that make poetic statements like this one: "Inside of one potato / there are mountains and rivers"?[4]

The point is obvious: the difficulty resides not in the nature of the *wasf*s but in the critical interpretation. The flaw
is not in the text but in the failure of scholars to appreciate
the very essence of metaphor, at the core of great poetry
from many eras and cultures. This essence is the extensive
psychic association that the poet Robert Bly calls "leaping":

> Thought of in terms of language, leaping is the ability to
> associate fast. In a great ancient or modern poem, the
> considerable distance between the associations, the dis-
> tance the spark has to leap, gives the lines their bottomless
> feeling, their space, and the speed of the association in-
> creases the excitement of the poetry.[5]

It is essentially this leap of the metaphor—the leap between the object and the image that describes it, that is, between tenor and vehicle—which troubles Bible scholars.
Richard Soulen, the author of the first passage quoted
above, points out that a fault with scholarly interpretation
lies in its literalistic approach.[6] This seems right, especially if
we understand literalism here to mean the need to find between tenor and vehicle a one-to-one correspondence in all
details. So Leroy Waterman, in the third passage quoted
above, cannot accept the metaphor of hair like a flock of
goats on a mountainside because the relation in size between
hairs and a head is not in proportion to that between goats
and a mountain.

The Wasf   At the other extreme, however, Soulen proposes to elim-
inate all visualizable correspondence between tenor and vehicle, arguing that this is what T. S. Eliot had in mind when
he spoke of the "objective correlative." Soulen writes:

> Its [the *wasf*'s] purpose is not to provide a parallel to vi-
> sual appearance or, as we shall see, primarily to describe
> feminine or masculine qualities metaphorically. The *ter-
> tium comparationis* must be seen instead in the feelings
> and sense experiences of the poet himself who then uses
> a vivid and familiar imagery to present to his hearers
> knowledge of those feelings in the form of art.

Soulen is right to note that the imagery in the *wasfs* is vivid
and familiar, for certainly it must have been so in the cultural
context of its time. But he offers little to make it similarly
vivid or familiar to us, since he declines to analyze it in its
particulars, to find in it *specific* objective correlatives for emotional experience. Rather, he concludes:

> That interpretation is most correct which sees the im-
> agery of the *wasf* as a means of arousing emotions con-
> sonant with those experienced by the suitor as he beholds
> the fullness of his beloved's attributes. . . . Just as the sen-
> sual experiences of love, beauty, and joy are vivid but in-
> effable, so the description which centers in and seeks to
> convey these very subjective feelings must for that reason
> be unanalytical and imprecise.

This is hardly a valid application of Eliot's principle, nor
is it an accurate description of what poetry does, for it fails
to address the question of *how* emotions are aroused in the
reader—how, finally, the ineffable ideal is conveyed through
words. By reducing the imagery in the *wasfs* to vague evo-
cations of ineffable feelings, Soulen deprives the relationship
between tenor and vehicle of all meaning. The point of comparison between a woman's hair and flocks of goats on a
mountainside lies, for him, "simply in the emotional congruity existing between two beautiful yet otherwise dispa-
rate sights." But if this were so, the poet might have chosen
any beautiful thing; there would hardly be a point to understanding this *particular* metaphor, or any other. Moreover, there would be no way to distinguish an apt metaphor

from a poor one, here or in any text, for as long as tenor and *The Wasf*
vehicle had vaguely similar emotional associations, the metaphor would hold true.

But one expects more of good poetry, and the Song ful-
fills these expectations. In fact, the metaphors in the Song express a sophisticated poetic sensibility that, although foreign
to us today, can be made accessible through a method of interpretive reading. This method consists of adopting the appropriate perspective, making explicit the implicit context,
filling in the unverbalized details.

Take the image that has so perturbed the scholars. When
one views the scene from a distance, the sight of goats winding down the slopes of the Israeli countryside is striking: the
dark animals weave a graceful pattern against the paler background of the hills. This image of contour and contrast may
thus suggest dark waves of hair cascading down a woman's
back. Similarly, a herd of sheep, emerging fresh from the
water, provides an ingenious metaphor when seen from afar:
the paired, white animals may call to mind twin rows of
white teeth. If this seems contrived to our sensibilities, we
should at least recognize that it is no more so than the Petrarchan convention comparing teeth to pearls. In fact, most
of the images in the *wasf*s are no more difficult to visualize
than the more familiar Petrarchan figures of speech found in
Renaissance poetry. With probing, even the most abstruse
images become clear. Consider the forehead behind the veil,
which is compared to a slice of pomegranate. It is puzzling
only at first; after reflecting on it with the mind's eye, we see
a gleam of red seeds through a net of white membrane.
Might this not be like rosy skin glimpsed through a mesh of
white veil? Once we see the image, we find it no more artificial—and no less artful—than the Petrarchan comparison
of cheeks to roses.

It is unnecessary and unfortunate to dismiss the images
of the *wasf* as either bizarre or imprecise. Meaningful interpretation lies between these extremes, in nonliteralistic visualization. Thus in translating the *wasf*s, when an image
required familiarity with a foreign landscape, I sometimes
suggested vantage points or settings that would allow mod-

The Wasf ern English readers to see in it what the original audience might have seen. Where the King James states, "Thy hair is as a flock of goats, that appear from mount Gilead," I rendered, "Your hair—/as black as goats/winding down the slopes," hinting at color and contour where they might otherwise be missed. For the same reason, I often eliminated proper place-names and substituted descriptions, as here in "the slopes" for "Mount Gilead" and, in another *wasf,* "two silent pools" for "pools in Heshbon," "the hills" for "Damascus," "majestic mountain" for "Carmel." (See "Four Basic Contexts" in chapter 5 for further discussion of place-names, and the note to poem 22 in chapter 6 for more information about these particular places.) When an image was not primarily visual, I tried to indicate its specific sensory appeal, as in "Lips like lilies, sweet / And wet with dew." Occasionally, to keep a metaphor from sounding hackneyed, I introduced a new detail, as in "Hair in waves of black / Like wings of ravens." Although wings are not mentioned in the original, neither is it likely that the Hebrew phrase "black as a raven" was, in its time, the cliché it has become in English today.

Thus the method of interpretive visualization often led me to lines that differ considerably from those in the standard translations. My goal was to let the images be vivid, not puzzling, pictures of a foreign but accessible culture, in hopes that the Song as a whole, and the *wasf*s in particular, might be demystified for both scholarly and general audiences.

※

Sometimes what is most mystifying, however, is not difficult at all—it is only challenging to our commonest expectations. Such is the case with female and male roles and images in the *wasf*—and indeed in the whole of the Song. As we shall see, this topic also leads to speculation concerning the Song's origins. The following passage from Soulen's article should help illuminate some of the problems with scholarly interpretation of the issue:

> The poetic imagination at work in 5:10–16 where the maiden speaks of her lover is less sensuous and imagina-

tive than in the *wasfs* of chapters 4 and 7 [where male
speakers describe females]. This is due in part to the limited subject matter and may even be due to the difference
in erotic imagination between poet and poetess.

The Wasf

Now let us look again at the text. A glance at the *wasf* in
5:10–16 (poem 19) reveals it to be no less sensuous and imaginative than any of the other *wasfs*. Soulen's evaluation,
then, perhaps derives from a preconception that the description of a man's body, as opposed to a woman's, is necessarily
"limited subject matter." Indeed, such a preconception may
not be surprising in a culture in which men are taught to believe that exaltation of male beauty is frivolous or, worse,
embarrassing. With such bias, any attempt to describe or
praise the male body would be doomed to fail. However, this
bias was hardly embedded in the poetic imagination of the
original text: there is nothing embarrassed about the female
voice speaking the *wasf,* and certainly nothing "limited" in
the description.

Soulen's further (literarily naive) assumption of a "poetess" behind the female persona is more surprising in context, because, like so many scholars, he refers in general to
the Song's author as male. There is a double prejudice at
work here. Throughout his article, Soulen speaks of the poet
in the masculine gender, seeming to disregard the possibility
that women may have contributed to the authorship of the
text. But when faced with a description of male beauty, he
assumes that the passage was composed by a female, at which
point he dismisses it as not warranting further study. (The
quoted statement comes from a footnote; Soulen never even
mentions this *wasf* again in his text.) Finally, he assumes that
"poet" and "poetess" have different (levels of? qualities of?)
"erotic imagination." The imagination of the "poetess" is,
for Soulen, not just different, but inferior; it is the possible
cause of a less lively poem.

Although this type of prejudicial attitude is, unfortunately, not unique among Bible scholars, Soulen's general
presumption of a male author for the Song is not shared by
all, and is today being challenged more than ever. One of the
first modern Bible scholars to question the notion was Goitein, who, in 1957, wrote: "Had we not received a tradition

The Wasf that King Solomon wrote this Song, we would say that a *woman* composed it. The book of the Song of Songs is a female composition, written from the point of view of the woman, not the man."[7] While it is not clear that Goitein is arguing explicitly for female authorship here, he seems at least to suggest that possibility, and without demeaning the Song's status because of it. Indeed, a decade later Goitein went on to develop his theory about the participation of women in biblical composition, particularly as poets, in a fascinating essay entitled "Women as Creators of Types of Literature in the Bible."[8] Largely as a result of feminist scholarship in the last two decades, Goitein's ideas seem less far-fetched to Bible scholars today than once they may have seemed.[9]

The allowance that women may have contributed to the Song's authorship seems more than reasonable, given what we know and what we may deduce of the Song's background. The supposition of an oral folk tradition assumes the participation of both women and men in composition and transmittal, and the main subject matter of the Song—erotic love—was certainly within the domain of women no less than men in ancient Israel. Moreover, as Bible scholar Carol Meyers points out, the Song's emphasis on the rural (that is, noninstitutional) and domestic domains (about which I will say more in the next chapter) reflects aspects of life in which women were primary.[10]

Indeed, the preponderance and authenticity of women's voices in the Song, as noted in chapter 3, may suggest a context of origin that is quite different from that of other biblical texts. In any case, it is clear that the Song itself, in sharp contrast to many of the critical voices that once surrounded it, offers a thoroughly nonsexist view of heterosexual love.[11] As we saw in our analysis of love monologues and dialogues, women in the Song speak as assertively as men, initiating action at least as often; so too, men are free to be as gentle, as vulnerable, even as coy as women. Not only in the *wasf*s but throughout the Song, men and women are mutually praised for their sensual appeal and beauty.

Consonant with this mutuality between the sexes, in the world of the Song no domination exists between human

beings and the rest of nature; rather, interrelationship pre-   *The Wasf*
vails. The presentation of natural phenomena as metaphors,
in the *wasf*s and elsewhere in the Song, and as contexts and
motifs (discussed in chapter 5) reveals a nonalienated and
nonnaive stance. Nature in the Song is neither idealized as
good nor subjugated—or demonized—because wild. Instead, it is depicted in the richness of its many manifesta-
tions, and always with respect for its power.

Sexist interpretation of the *wasf,* then, and of the Song
in general, is a striking example of how the text can be distorted by culturally biased reading. To interpret the Song
with integrity, we must shed the cultural blinders that make
what is foreign seem strange. It may turn out that this ancient text has something new to teach about the redemption
of sexuality and love in our fallen world.[12]

CHAPTER 5

Contexts, Themes,
and Motifs

WOVEN INTO THE TAPESTRY of the Song are recurrent patterns that suggest the presence of literary conventions, analogous in some ways to the Petrarchan conventions of
Renaissance poetry. To uncover and illuminate recurrent
material in the Song may draw us closer to the distant cultural source of this poetry, while also deepening our appreciation of the individual poems and of the collection as a
whole. The following discussions are intended to reveal patterns in the text by illuminating settings and ambiance
(which I call "contexts"), underlying premises and ideas
("themes"), and repeated images and symbols ("motifs").
These categories were not fixed in my mind prior to translating; rather, they emerged during the process and, especially, afterwards, when I was able to step back from the text
once again and see its contours from a new vantage point.

*Contexts,
Themes,
and Motifs*

❧ FOUR BASIC CONTEXTS

Context as setting is not equally dominant in all the poems
of the Song; some poems depend crucially on setting for
their arguments or moods, while others seem not to "take
place" anywhere in particular, but to focus more on internal
(psychological) space. Yet even when the setting of a poem
is undefined, ambiance or atmosphere is present to some degree. Context changes often in the Song, from poem to
poem and sometimes within poems, creating kaleidoscopic
shifts of pattern. Out of this movement we can isolate four
basic contexts that, either separately or in combination,
color most of the poems in the Song:

  (a) the cultivated or habitable countryside;
  (b) the wild or remote natural landscape and its
      elements;
  (c) interior environments (houses, halls, rooms);
  (d) city streets.

  (a) All the love dialogues and many of the love monologues take place, at least in part, in the countryside. The pastures of poem 3, the grove of poem 6, the valley and thicket
of poem 7, the blossoming spring landscapes of poems 9, 21,
and 24, the rocks and ravines of poem 10, the hills of poems

12, 15, and 31, the gardens of poems 18, 19, and 31, and the shade of the quince tree in poem 27 are all tempting and conducive sites for love. Either of the lovers may take the initiative in these settings, which themselves seem to invite lovemaking. The poems that share these lush pastoral contexts tend to portray young, idealized love: the pleasure of anticipation finds at least as much expression here as does the experience of fulfillment. Although the lovers are often separated in the countryside, reunions are expected. Thus, in the benign and receptive rural landscape, invitations to love are playful, suffused with feelings of happy arousal.

The countryside also sets the scene, as background if not foreground, for other types of poems—2, 11, and 30—that are not love monologues or dialogues. In each of these, the country is represented by the vineyard, a special kind of place (discussed below as a separate motif). As we have already observed and shall presently see further, the tone of these poems is quite different from that of the love monologues just mentioned.

(b) Although nature is generally receptive to the human lovers of the Song, another kind of natural context lends a very different ambiance to several poems. This is the landscape of wild, remote, sometimes dangerous nature: the desert/wilderness of poems 14 and 26, the mountain lairs of poem 16, the seas and rivers of poem 28, and the staring eye of the heavens in poems 2 and 20. These elements of nature suggest distant or overwhelming forces, which evoke anxiety or a sense of urgency, as in poems 16 and 28, or create a miragelike atmosphere, as in poems 14 and 26, or suggest mystery, as in poems 2 and 20. Although these natural elements are sometimes central images rather than complete settings, their effect in the poems is always strong; the poems that share this ambiance have a different mood from others in the collection, a mood permeated by awe. In contrast to the countryside setting, this context does not support intimacy; here nature can keep the lovers apart or be a fearsome backdrop to their union. The expression of love is not playful but reverent, sometimes even overwhelmed. Not just *I-Thou* love is expressed in this context, but a variety of emotional experiences, balancing the more predictable range found in the countryside.

(c) Interior environments take several forms in the Song—the king's chambers in poems 1 and 5, the winehall in poem 8, the speaker's bedroom in poems 13 and 19, and the mother's house in poems 13 and 25—all associated with love-making. In addition, poem 9 opens with a woman inside her house, listening for the voice of her lover, and poem 24 closes with an anticipated return from the countryside to the doorways of the lovers' home, where, the speaker promises, the lovemaking will reach its climax. The interior environment often encourages the modes of dreams and fantasies, and the imagination seems to have its freest reign here.

Associated twice with the interior context of the home is the figure of the mother. The mother's house is the most intimate and protected environment in the Song; for this reason, the speakers of poems 13 and 25 want to lead their beloveds out of the streets and back to this private place, where they will be completely free to express their love.

The supportive bond of love between mother and child, which is implied in these poems (and in others not set in this context: 14, 20, 27), is in sharp contrast to some of the sibling relationships portrayed in the Song. In poem 2, for example, the "mother's sons" seem to have punished their sister for being sexually active; again in 29, the brothers want to protect their sister from, or punish her for, having erotic experience (see the note to poem 29 in chapter 6). Siblings, however, are not always portrayed as hostile; in poem 25 the speaker says that *if* her lover *were* her brother, she would feel free to kiss him in the public streets, which implies that sibling affection, besides being considered natural, is assumed by the speaker to be socially acceptable. And of course, the metaphorical phrase "my sister, my bride" (poems 17 and 18) also suggests that affection was an inherent aspect of sibling relationships (see the note to poem 17 in chapter 6).

Strikingly, no mention of a father—or of the father's home—appears anywhere in the Song.[1] Rather, male figures (with the exception of male lovers, and "the king" when used as a metaphor for the lover) play more distant roles,

Contexts,
Themes,
and Motifs
making their appearances in more public contexts. Public society, as we shall see next, creates a sharply different context
from the microcosm of the home.

(d) Of all the contexts of the Song, the public domain
of the city is the one least sympathetic to the lovers. Thus the
city watchmen, or guards, are of no help to the woman
searching for her beloved in poem 13; in poem 19 these same
figures violate the female lover. The speaker of poem 25
senses the city's danger: she knows she cannot kiss her beloved in the streets without exposing herself to ridicule. The
city women (literally, "daughters of Jerusalem" or "daughters of Zion") are another group of spectators whose attitude toward the lovers is less than sympathetic: in poems 8,
13, and 25 they must be adjured not to disturb the lovemaking; in poem 19 they offer to help the woman find her beloved only after she entices them with a description of his
charms. In poem 2, the city women are the hostile audience
of a rural woman whose dark beauty they scorn. (In poem
14, the only other poem in which the daughters of Jerusalem
appear, they play a different role. This poem is set in the desert rather than the city, and the women here are associated
not with the public streets but with the entourage of the
king. I have therefore distinguished them in this context by
referring to them, in a more literal translation, as "Jerusalem's daughters.") Like the city guards, the city women provide a foil against which the intimate world-of-two emerges
as an ideal; their presence contributes to the conflict and tension that often emerge in poems having urban settings. (I
shall explore these ideas further in the ensuing discussions of
themes.)

Related to the subject of contexts are proper place-
names, which appear frequently in the Hebrew text. In Hebrew these names often have considerable resonance, but in
translation they lose a great deal. The places named in the
Hebrew include Jerusalem/Zion, Ein Gedi, Lebanon,
Mount Gilead, Amana, Senir, Hermon, Tirza, Heshbon,
Bat-Rabbim, Damascus, Carmel, and Baal-Hamon. I re-

tained specific names in the translations when I thought they had clear associations for a contemporary English reader, or when I felt that specificity added to, rather than detracted from, the point of the poem. For example, in poem 20 I chose to use the names "Tirza" and "Jerusalem" instead of referring generally to "cities," because the musicality of the one, alongside the familiarity of the other, contributed, I felt, to the poem's atmosphere. More often than not, though, I interpreted the meanings of place-names for the English reader, as in the example of "the slopes" for Mount Gilead (cited in chapter 4). I did not strive for consistency in making these choices; as elsewhere, my decisions were based on the demands of the individual poems and what I believed would allow maximum expression in English verse.

Contexts, Themes, and Motifs

✸ FIVE THEMES AND THEIR VARIATIONS

The themes I analyze here were isolated for various reasons: to point out conceptual connections among poems, to explain otherwise enigmatic material, and to illuminate the intellectual and emotional fabric from which the poems in the Song are cut. This analysis does not attempt to cover all the thematic material in the Song, but treats instead what plays a significant, though not necessarily obvious, role. The following five themes not only recur but overlap, representing interwoven threads of meaning in over half the poems of the Song:

(a) beckoning the beloved (poems 1, 9, 10, 16, 24, 31);
(b) banishing the beloved—the theme of secret love (poems 12, 15, 31);
(c) searching for the beloved (poems 3, 13, 19);
(d) the self in a hostile world (poems 2, 29, 30);
(e) praise of love itself (poems 23, 28).

(a) Beckoning the beloved, a classic theme in the Western courtly love tradition, is central to many of the love monologues and dialogues in the Song. Unlike the poetry of courtly love, however, in the Song both female and male speakers beckon—or make invitations to—the beloved. As might be expected, beckoning is often accompanied by

Contexts,
Themes,
and Motifs

praise; as a part of courting, beckoning is enhanced by the lavishing of compliments. Poems that share this theme portray the idealism and romanticism of courtship and often have a mood of wondrous expectation about them. Their tone tends to be flirtatious and often coy, though sometimes they are also quite passionate.

The literary devices used to beckon the beloved are various. Sometimes praise and entreaties suffice, as in poems 1, 10, and 31. The speakers of poems 9 and 24 describe the lush countryside in an effort to induce their beloveds to join them there. The argument of these poems is that of the classic spring song: all of nature is mating—why not we too? Poem 16, in contrast, depicts an ominous landscape; the speaker urges his beloved to leave the danger, to "come away" with him.

A linguistic feature associated with the theme of beckoning is the frequent use of verbal imperatives. "Take me away" (literally, "pull me") says the speaker of poem 1. In poems 9, 10, 16, and 24, the speakers use verbal imperatives to extend invitations, which I rendered consistently with the verb "come." I chose this verb in part to suggest thematic similarity among these poems, and partly because more literal translations ("get up," "show me," "go") lack the delicate evocativeness of the Hebrew. The first half of poem 31, which also uses an imperative, seemed to me so imploring in tone that I rendered the imperative as a request: "will you let me hear you?"

In part, the pathos of these poems derives from the pain of the implied separation of the lovers and the strength of their desire to be united. Again, as distinct from the later poetry of the Western tradition, in these poems emotions are shared equally by both lovers, and may be expressed at different moments by either one of them. This mutuality only intensifies the pathos of separation in the Song. Separation is involved in other themes as well, and is crucial, as we shall see next, to the theme of secret love.

(b) In poems 12 and 15 and in the second half of 31, the male lover/beloved either is chased away or voluntarily leaves the woman. Poems 12 and 31 may seem particularly puzzling, because the female speaker refers to her beloved with an endearing love name as she banishes him. In poem 31, she is responding to her lover's tender invitation, and one hardly expects her to be unsympathetic. In fact, in neither poem is her tone angry or even aloof; yet she is firm in her commands: as in the passages of beckoning, verbal imperatives are used ("turn round" and "go," in my translation). What are we to make of this?

The key to these poems lies, I believe, in viewing the romance as secret, an affair that can be consummated only at night, when the lovers are not exposed to public scrutiny. By chasing her beloved away in poems 12 and 31, the woman is not rejecting him, only exercising caution. The male speaker acts from the same motivation at the close of poem 15.

This interpretation accounts for otherwise enigmatic statements that most standard Bible translations attempt to circumvent. For example, in the second stanza of poem 31 the female speaker responds to her lover's invitation with the rather abrupt-sounding command *b⁽rah,* which means, literally, "flee." Perhaps because this seems, on first reading, out of tone with the rest of the passage, the standard translations alter the meaning: the King James and Revised Standard Versions render *b⁽rah* as "make haste," and *The New American Bible* reads "come into the open." But there is no mistaking the meaning of the biblical Hebrew text. The word *b⁽rah* is neither rare nor ambiguous; it means not "come" or even "make haste," but "run away—flee."

So too, in the second stanza of poem 12, the female speaker tells her beloved to *sov*—literally, "turn," the implication being "turn away from me." *Sov,* in this passage, seems to be analogous to *b⁽rah* in poem 31, as we can see from reading further in each poem. Both commands are followed by elaborate instructions from the speakers: lines reading, literally, "make yourself, my beloved, like a gazelle or young stag on the split mountains" in poem 12, and "my beloved, make yourself like a gazelle or young stag on the mountains of spices" in poem 31. These lines—so similar as to sound almost like a refrain—seem to link the meaning and intention of the women's speech in the two poems.

Finally, the same Hebrew lines that precede *sov* in poem 12—literally, "until the day breathes and the shadows disappear" (in my translation, "Until the day is over / And the shadows flee")—also precede the statement made by the male speaker at the end of poem 15. In the latter, the speaker *voluntarily* resolves to go away to the mountains / hills (here they are "the mountain of myrrh" and "the hill of frankincense," rendered together in my translation as "the hills / of fragrant bloom") "until the day breathes and the shadows disappear" (in my translation, "Until / the day is over, / shadows gone"). Thus, the closing of poem 15 seems also to be linked to the endings of poems 12 and 31; indeed, the situation of all three passages seems the same. In all three, the male lover is expected to remove himself from his beloved by running away to the hills; but the qualifying phrase "until the day is over" in poems 12 and 15 limits the duration of the separation. Underlying the explicit speech of all three poems is the unspoken understanding that the man will return to his beloved later—at night, when they will be out of public view.

My reading of the phrase "until the day breathes" as "until the day is over" supports the above interpretation. Some scholars, however, take this phrase to mean "until the day breaks." Mine, I believe, is the simpler reading, in that it assumes the shadows are ordinary sun-shadows whose departure suggests day's end. Moreover, in a hot Mediterranean climate the day indeed seems to breathe at dusk, when the afternoon wind rises and the air begins to cool.

Additional support for finding the theme of secret love is contained in the double entendres of these poems. The mountains / hills—whether fragrant or split—may be read as metaphors for the woman's body, just as the gazelle / stag may be seen as a metaphor for the man. Thus, on the metaphorical level, at the very moment of separation the lovers' reunion is prefigured.

In our discussion of contexts, we saw that the public domain is unsympathetic to the lovers and that the city is the setting most threatening to the love relationship. Now we see that sometimes even in the countryside, where both male and female speakers express the desire to meet, the lovers feel that their rendezvous must be kept secret, confined to night-time. This may be because of fear of public censure, or it may be a kind of fiction, part of a lovers' game. In either case, the theme of secret love explains otherwise baffling statements in at least three poems in the Song, and may deepen our understanding of other poems as well. For example, beckoning may now be seen as a counterpoint to secrecy: one lover coaxes while the other cautiously hides away. This explains the shyness or coyness of the hidden lover, and the fervor of the one extending the invitation.

Contexts, Themes, and Motifs

The role of the public, as it relates to the theme of secret love, has implications for the interpretation of yet other kinds of poems. It is especially important to the next two themes.

(c) Searching for the beloved is the explicit theme of poems 13 and 19. Both poems open in the bedroom and then move into the city streets, where the speaker encounters the public world. In her search for her beloved, the female speaker of each poem first comes upon the city watchmen, who in poem 13 are unresponsive, and in poem 19 are actually brutal. These are the only two poems in which the figures of the guards appear, and it is difficult to speculate about their actual role in society. However, as representatives of the public domain—groups of people outside the love relationship—they conform to a general pattern in the Song: they represent the real world, so to speak, against which the ideal world-of-two is contrasted.

The city women constitute another such group that appears in several poems of the Song. Although never as threatening as the male guards, these figures are often aloof and sometimes hostile spectators, situated outside the love relationship. When their aid is solicited to find the lost beloved in poem 19, they respond at first with reluctance and suspicion, as if to say: what's so special about your lover that we should bother to help you find him? But after the woman replies with a lengthy and detailed description of him, the women are eager to participate in the search. At this point, the speaker turns them away, affirming that she knows where

147

Contexts,
Themes,
and Motifs to find her beloved after all. The closing of this poem suggests that the search for the beloved, frenzied though it seems, may be only a fiction or a game. In other terms, the search may be a metaphorical way of describing the loss that is felt whenever the beloved is not near, even if his whereabouts are known. Alternatively, the conclusion of the poem may be a bluff, or a desperate fantasy or wish. In either case, when the city women are ready to offer help, they are perceived as intruders. This perception may also explain why, in poem 13, the women are adjured not to wake or rouse the lovers, that is, not to disturb them in their lovemaking (for a more detailed explanation of this adjuration, see the note to poem 8 in chapter 6).

If we take the view that the urban searches in poems 13 and 19 are fictions or metaphors for feelings of loss, rather than actual odysseys into the streets, we may gain insight into the pastoral search that is the theme of poem 3. Here the speaker directly addresses her beloved with the request to know where she can find him while he is tending his flock, which is to say, during the daytime. The question, one deduces, is asked at night when the lovers are together and by themselves. The tone of the dialogue is coy rather than frantic, which is appropriate to a lovers' game. It is misguided to find the response of the male speaker cold or harshly evasive. The question itself is asked playfully, and the response implies that the woman is not really in need of an answer: "*If you don't know*," says the man—implying that she knows perfectly well where he may be found.

While the woman addresses her beloved directly in this poem, she also makes reference to other individuals outside the intimate relationship. She does not, she says, want to go about begging directions from her lover's friends. The friends here play a role similar to that of the city women in other poems. Though they may not be hostile, neither can they be expected to be of much help. They too represent the public domain, which is repeatedly in conflict with the lovers' wish to be united.

(d) In poems 2 and 30, which make symbolic reference to erotic experience but are not specifically addressed to the

beloved, we see yet another aspect of the role of figures out- *Contexts,*
side the love relationship. Both these poems are monologues *Themes,*
addressed to representatives of the public domain: the city *and Motifs*
women in one instance, King Solomon in the other. While
neither Solomon nor the city women speak in these poems,
we are invited to deduce their attitudes from the defiant and
even indignant tones of the monologues.

The purpose of the postures struck by the speakers of
these poems is self-assertion; both speakers present themselves in contrast to the outside world. Thus in poem 2, the
speaker asserts that she is black *and* beautiful, even though
others—the city women—may consider her dark skin un-
attractive. In poem 30, the speaker argues that his vineyard—a symbol for his beloved — is more valuable to him
than the vineyard of the king. In both poems, the security
provided by the love relationship gives the speakers confi-
dence and even a measure of audacity, with which they are
able to confront the public world.

Similarly, the female speaker in the dialogue poem 29 replies to the speech of her overprotective brothers with a declaration of her lover's regard for her. The men in this poem
seem to have a punitive attitude toward their younger sister,
who responds to them with a proud defiance of their au-
thority. (The brothers referred to in poem 2 may have a similar attitude toward their sister.)

Indignation, defiance, fear, and hostility are emotions
that have their parts in the Song, emerging often, as we have
seen, in connection with the public domain. We find in the
Song that self-love, like love of the other, meets often with
challenges from the outside world but finds constant support
in the intimate world-of-two.

(e) Explicit in only two poems, but implied in almost all
the poems in the collection, is praise of love itself. As the
opening lines of poem 23 exclaim, "Of all pleasure, how
sweet / Is the taste of love!" While poem 23 does not pursue
this thought explicitly, shifting instead to praise of the beloved, poem 28 is devoted almost entirely to praise of love.
In this sense, poem 28 is unique in the collection, and distinguishes itself further by its use of hyperbole and singular

imagery. It is the only poem in the Song that mentions death, pitting death against love in a contest for power. Love does not necessarily conquer death, the poem expounds, but neither is it conquered by it. Love blazes despite all attempts to put it out.

The opening lines of poem 23 and the middle stanzas of poem 28 make two different statements about love: whereas the one proclaims the sensual joy of love, the other asserts its power. These two appreciations represent the emotional range of the text. The themes treated above indicate that the fabric of the Song is not smooth and even-textured, but knotted with tension and struggle. These aspects of particular love relationships are proclaimed to be the nature of love itself in poems 23 and 28. Taken as a whole, the Song eloquently expresses some of the paradoxes of erotic love: conflict that intensifies passion, painful separation that heightens the pleasure of union, intimate bonding with the other that gives the individual courage to stand alone.

❧ SIX CENTRAL MOTIFS

Interwoven among the dominant themes of the Song are other, more delicate strands of meaning: images and symbols embroidered into the design of the tapestry. These are what I call motifs; the following recur most often and seem most prominent:

(a) flora and fauna, and artifice, as complementary sources of imagery;
(b) the vines and the vineyard, as a special place and as metaphors and symbols;
(c) the garden, as a special place and as an extended metaphor;
(d) eating and drinking as erotic metaphors;
(e) regality and wealth, as metaphors, figures, and foils;
(f) sensuality and the senses.

(a) The references to flora and fauna in the Song are so many and various that the Song has come to be thought of as nature poetry. It is true that "'nature poetry' is a clumsy term," as the poet Wendell Berry points out, "for there is a sense in which most poetry is nature poetry; most poets, even those least interested in nature, have found in the world an abundant stock of symbols and metaphors."[2] But in the Song, flora and fauna are essential: they abound everywhere, in foregrounds and backgrounds, as real, metaphorical, and symbolic. Plants and animals appear as depictions of the natural landscape (as in poems 3, 6, 9, 16, 19, 21, 24, 27, and 31), as metaphors for the beloved (for example, in poems 4, 5, 7, 9, 10, 12, 18, 23, and 31), and as metaphors for parts of the human body (the best examples of these are in the *wasfs*). The animals in the Song include the mare, dove, gazelle, deer, nightingale ("songbird," in my translation), turtledove ("dove," in my translation), fox, lion, leopard, and raven. Most of these are identifiable by their biblical Hebrew names, although the standard English Bibles give somewhat differing translations for a few—for example, "stag" or "hart" for deer, "jackal" for fox. The plants mentioned in the Song are even more numerous—over twenty-five varieties of trees, shrubs, flowers, herbs, fruits, nuts, spices, and nectars—and their identification is more problematic. Because botanical images are so numerous and recurrent in the Song, I will comment on their identification, interpretation, and translation before discussing their relationship to the world of artifice.

Like most botanical references in the Bible, those in the Song are difficult to identify because their biblical names do not necessarily correspond to modern Hebrew usage. For example, while today the word *tappuah* means "apple," it must have referred to something else in biblical times, because apples were not indigenous to ancient Israel. The translations in standard English Bibles and other versions of the Song tend to be misleading because the translators have hardly investigated the original referents of biblical plant names. And when modern versions do depart from the traditional renderings, they often do no more than guess at the meaning of these words; they rarely go so far as to attempt to determine the impact these images might have had in their original poetic contexts.

I believe that faithful translation of botanical imagery in the Song has three stages: first, accurate identification of the referent of the biblical Hebrew plant name, to the extent

Contexts, Themes, and Motifs

Contexts,
Themes,
and Motifs

possible; second, interpretation of the effect of the image in its original poetic context; finally, choice of an English word or phrase that will both evoke the original landscape and have an analogous effect in the new context of the English poem.

I was greatly assisted in the first stage by the findings of the research institute Neot Kedumim (the Gardens of Israel). The staff members at Neot Kedumim have done important work in the field of biblical botany; by consulting native speakers of languages that are cognate with Hebrew but that, unlike Hebrew, have retained the same common botanical names over the centuries, they have succeeded in identifying many of the plants named in the Bible. In addition, by cultivating and studying the terrain of present-day Israel, they have been able to make reasonable conjectures about the vegetation of biblical times. I considered the information provided by Neot Kedumim to be authoritative in most cases, and I used it as the basis for the next two stages, the interpretation of effect and the choice of English analogues.

I applied my overall approach to interpretation and translation, discussed in previous chapters, to my translations of botanical imagery. For example, when a flower was used in the Song as a metaphor, I tried first to determine the point of the comparison: was it visual beauty, or fragrance, or perhaps texture that was being called to mind? I then searched for an equivalent image in English, one that would have similar impact on the modern reader. When using specific names, I tried, as often as possible, to name in English the same plants referred to in the Hebrew; but if these plants had accrued, over the centuries, inappropriate associations (as with myrrh and frankincense), or if the English names sounded archaic or otherwise awkward, I found alternate expressions. In addition, I sometimes substituted descriptions for specific names (such as "sweet fruit tree growing wild" for *tappuaḥ;* see the note to poem 7 in chapter 6) and sometimes named plants of related species or having similar characteristics. I did not translate botanical images consistently from poem to poem, but let the demands of the individual poems guide my decisions. For example, I translated the oft-mentioned *šošannah* (narcissus) at different moments as "narcissus," "lily," "daffodil," "wildflower," and sometimes simply "flower"; in some cases I used different translations within a single poem, in order to stress a particular point in English (see, for example, poem 7 and the note to it in chapter 6). Although I translated these images with considerable flexibility, I tried throughout to respect the integrity of the original landscape by never naming plants that could not have been part of it; I also did not name plants that would be totally unfamiliar to modern English readers.

The decisions I made in translating botanical images were especially difficult because these images, more than most others, convey specific, culture-bound information that resists migration. Plants tend not to be hardy travelers, so one must take pains when carrying them across to new terrain, lest their vitality be endangered.

Although plant and animal images are found throughout the Song, they are by no means the exclusive source of metaphor. Even in the *wasf*s, which rely heavily on natural imagery, metaphors are drawn from the realms of artifice—art, craft, and architecture—and these seem to mingle freely with metaphors from nature. Thus in the *wasf* of poem 19, the man's hair is black as a raven, his eyes are like doves, his cheeks like spices, his lips like flowers, and his stature or appearance like cedars in the mountains; but his arms are cylinders of gold studded with jewels, his belly is a slab of ivory inlaid with gems, and his legs are marble columns set on gold stands—all images evoking sculptural and architectural forms. Similarly, in the *wasf* of poem 15, the woman's lips are like threads of silk and her neck like a tower adorned with shields, images of artifice and architecture that are interspersed among images from nature—doves, goats, sheep, pomegranates, fawns. So too in the *wasf* of poem 22, thighs like spinning jewels suggest the artisan's handicraft, and the towerlike neck and face connote architectural grandeur, but the natural landscape—of wheat, flowers, pools, and mountains—lends images for other parts of the body.[3]

In addition, the artifice of military society provides images for some poems in the Song. The tower in poem 15 is hung with the shields of warriors; the wall, door, and turrets of poem 29 suggest the structure of a fortress; sixty sword-bearing warriors in poem 14 attend the procession of the king. It is fascinating to note that military imagery in the Song applies more often to descriptions of a female than of a male—one more example of the Song's reversal of our stereotypical expectations.[4]

Finally, the argument of poem 4 makes explicit what is implied throughout the Song: while the beloved is perceived as naturally beautiful, the speaker sees no harm in adding artificial adornment; artifice does not compete with nature but complements it. Similar to other contrasts we have observed—such as between public and private domains or separation and union of lovers—the relationship between the natural world and the world of human artifacts is mutually intensifying and contributes to the density of the Song's texture.

(b) The words *gefen,* "vine," and *kerem,* "vineyard," appear in eight poems in the Song, often more than once in each. I have translated these words in various ways—"vine," "vineyard," "grapevine," "grapes"—depending on the needs of the English poems. For the sake of this discussion, however, I will revert to a stricter distinction between the two Hebrew words. *Gefen* appears in poems 9, 21, 23, and 24; *kerem,* in poems 2, 5, 11, 24, and 30.

In poems 9, 21, and 24, *gefen* refers to the grapevine in the stage of budding or early fruit, when it gives forth fragrance. All three of these poems are spring songs, and the *gefen* is one of the details in the springtime landscape. In all three, moreover, the budding vines are associated with erotic experience, invited or anticipated by one of the lovers. In poem 23, *gefen* appears in the phrase *ešk⁼lot haggefen,* "clusters of the vine"; here the reference is to the mature fruit, and I have rendered it "clusters of grapes." The poet evokes the smooth round fruit of the vine as a metaphor for the beloved's breasts.

The word *kerem* is also used in various ways. In poem 24 it refers to a vineyard, which, like the fields where the henna blooms, is an appealing site for the lovers. In poem 5 it is associated with Ein Gedi, where, according to the poem, *kofer,*

"henna" ("blossoms," in my translation), is found. Because
Ein Gedi is an oasis in the desert and henna does not grow
on vines, the *kerem* of poem 5 seems to be not a vineyard but
a general place of vegetation; I have rendered it here as
"oasis."

While in both poems 5 and 24 *kerem* refers to a place of
vegetation, a wider range of meanings is suggested in poems
2, 11, and 30, because it is impossible to interpret these poems
coherently without a symbolic reading. In each of these
poems, *kerem* is mentioned several times, and once in each it
is in the first-person possessive: "my vineyard" in poems 2
and 30, "our vineyards" in poem 11. In poems 2 and 30 an emphatic modifier, *šelli*, "mine," follows the possessive *karmi*,
"my vineyard"; I have indicated this emphatically possessive
construction in the English with the phrase "my own." The
female speaker of poem 2 says that she has been made to
watch the vineyards (although the Hebrew does not specify
whose these are, we may deduce from the context that they
belong to the speaker's brothers), and meanwhile she has not
watched her own. The male speaker of poem 30 says that Solomon has a prosperous vineyard but that his, the speaker's,
own vineyard is more precious to him than Solomon's. Both
poems suggest that the vineyard is to be understood as more
than a literal place; at least when referred to in the possessive
form, it seems to be also a symbol for female sexuality. Thus
when the woman speaks of her own vineyard, she refers to
herself; when the man speaks of his own vineyard, he refers
to his beloved. In poem 2, the woman alludes to not having
guarded her own sexuality; in poem 30, the speaker asserts
that his beloved is not to be shared with anyone else.

Poem 11 contains the most cryptic of all the references to
kerem, because here it is unclear who is speaking and to
whom. But once again the poem makes most sense if we understand the *kerem* symbolically: the foxes (a masculine noun
in the Hebrew) are raiding the vineyards and therefore must
be caught; if the "little foxes" are young men, might the
vineyards be young women?

It should not be disconcerting to find *kerem* used in several different ways in the collection. The accumulated mean-

ings enhance the resonance of each occurrence of the motif, and from this layering comes textural richness.

(c) The garden, like the vineyard, appears in several different poems in the Song, sometimes as a location and sometimes as a metaphor for the female beloved. Even when it refers to a location, however, it is generally associated with the woman, and it sometimes simultaneously symbolizes her.

In poem 31, the garden is the place where the female beloved is situated; in the penultimate stanza of poem 19, it is a place entered by a male. The walnut orchard of poem 21 is literally a "walnut garden," to which the speaker "goes down" ("walking," in my translation) to observe the opening of the flowers. In poem 19, the male beloved "has gone down" ("has gone to walk," in my translation) to "his garden" to feed his sheep and gather flowers. The links between these two passages—the same verb and the similar references to flowers or flowering—make a strong argument for viewing the otherwise unidentifiable speaker of poem 21 as male. The association of the garden with the female beloved in poem 31 further suggests a symbolic level of meaning in poems 19 and 21: the garden represents the female beloved, who is "gone down to" by the male; the gathering and eating of flowers may be read as the male's erotic play on the woman's body, and the opening of the flowers as the woman's erotic response.

In poem 18, the garden is *explicitly* erotic, functioning as an extended metaphor that describes the beloved. The word *gan,* "garden," appears five times in the Hebrew poem, three times in the possessive ("my garden" and "his garden"). Like the vineyard in poems 2 and 30, the garden in poem 18 can belong to either the woman or the man, but it seems to refer in both cases to the woman herself or to her sexuality. Thus the female speaker calls upon the winds to breathe on *ganni,* "my garden," invoking her beloved to come to *ganno,* "his garden." The two references are, of course, to the same garden, and to avoid confusion in the English I omitted the phrase "his garden" here. In the following stanza, the male

speaker replies that he has come to "my garden," thus ac-
cepting the gift that the woman has offered.

As in poem 19, the male speaker in poem 18 gathers
plants (this time spices rather than flowers) in his garden,
and also feasts there. Because poem 18 is controlled by an extended metaphor in which the female is compared to the garden itself, to the water that flows in it, and to all the varieties
of vegetation (fruits, flowers, woods, spices) that grow in it,
the activities of the male in the garden—entering, gathering, and eating—are also to be seen as erotic. The use of the
garden as an extended metaphor here (analyzed in more detail in the note to poem 18 in chapter 6) suggests ways to view
the motif of eating and drinking in other poems as well.

(d) The Hebrew word-root *'kl*, "eat," appears three
times in the Song, all in poem 19, where I have translated it
variously as "share," "taste," and "feast"—verbs that build in
intensity as they approach the poem's climax. The female
speaker in the poem expresses the wish that her beloved will
come to his garden and eat ("share") its choice fruits; the
male speaker replies that he has come to gather spices, to eat
("taste") his honey and drink his wine and milk. At the conclusion of the poem, a third voice invites the two lovers to
eat ("feast") and drink, even to the point of intoxication
("drink deeply," in my translation). Clearly, eating and
drinking are symbols of erotic experience; the association of
eating and drinking with the garden, and with the activity
of gathering in particular, suggests that eroticism is implied
also in other settings where eating and drinking occur.

For example, in the penultimate stanza of poem 19, the
woman says that her beloved has gone down to his garden
lir'ot, "to pasture" (in my version, "to feed his sheep"), and
to gather flowers. In the last stanza she refers to him as *haro'eh
baššošannim*, "the one who pastures among the flowers," an
appellation that appears in poem 12 as well (I translate the
phrase, in both instances, "Who leads his flock to feed /
Among the flowers"). The Hebrew word for pasturing, or
feeding one's flocks, also appears in poem 3: there the female
speaker asks her beloved where he pastures ("where you feed

*Contexts,
Themes,
and Motifs*

Contexts,
Themes,
and Motifs

your sheep," in my version), and the male speaker replies by telling her to pasture her own flocks among the fields of the other "ones who pasture" ("the shepherds," in my translation). In all these cases where the word-root *r'h* appears, there is an implied second level of meaning. Because pasturing is associated with the garden, with flowers, and with gathering—all of which have erotic connotations, the more so when they appear in combination—there is the strong suggestion that pasturing means not only feeding one's flock but feeding oneself in the act of love. Because the garden and its flowers are, as we have seen, often associated with the female body, pasturing is usually symbolic of male sexual activity. The one who pastures in the flowers is always a male (although poem 3 contains a reference to a woman who pastures, flowers are not mentioned in that instance).

Other, more direct references to the activities of eating and drinking, however, are not restricted to males; these too have erotic associations. In poem 7, the female speaker says that her beloved's fruit is sweet to her palate ("I taste your love," in my translation); here the male is compared to a fruit tree, and the speaker finds pleasure in dwelling in his shadow and tasting his fruit. In poem 8, the female speaker asks to be refreshed and sustained with raisincakes and quinces—an unusual request from one who is "sick with love." It seems that her hunger is not so much for cakes and fruits as for her lover's embrace, about which she fantasizes in the succeeding lines.

The food in the Song most emphatically associated with lovemaking is wine. More than once it is mentioned by way of complimenting a beloved: for example, that her mouth is like good wine (poem 23), or that her lovemaking is better than wine (poem 17), or that *his* lovemaking is better than wine (poem 1). The speaker of poem 17 goes on to praise his beloved in detail, not failing to mention the taste of honey and milk on her tongue, thus making explicit the association between lovemaking and food. Honey and milk (probably a "fixed pair," a convention of oral poetry) are linked with wine in poem 18 as well. In both poems, honey and milk lend added sweetness to the imagery of the wine and reinforce its erotic overtones.

The imagery of wine is perhaps nowhere more erotic, however, than in poem 25, where it is in parallel position to the nectar of pomegranates. The speaker of this poem offers to take her beloved to her mother's home, where she will give him spiced wine and the juice of her pomegranate to drink. The pomegranate, long recognized as a fertility symbol in ancient culture, is mentioned in connection with females several times in the Song: as a fruit of the gardens in poems 18 and 21, and as a metaphor for the woman's forehead in the *wasfs*. In poem 25 it seems to be a symbol, like the vineyard, of the woman's sexuality, an image that the first-person possessive, "my pomegranate," emphasizes. The lines that follow are the same those that follow the request for food in poem 8 (which, incidentally, takes place in a winehall); and in both instances, the allusions to feasting lead into the woman's fantasy of her beloved's embrace. Feasting, it seems, always has erotic overtones in the Song, and wine is the intoxicating temptation to the feast.

(e) Like the other motifs discussed here, regality is treated in various ways in the Song, but unlike the others, its connotations can be either positive or negative. Thus when the beloved is compared to a king, as in poems 1 and 5, the regal image is clearly a compliment, a way of expressing affection and esteem. This is also the effect of calling the woman a princess in poem 22, and of stating, in the same poem, that she captures kings in the tresses of her hair—as if to say that her beauty is capable of attracting *anyone*. In poem 2, the image of King Solomon's tapestries also has positive associations: it is a metaphor for the speaker's black and lovely skin.

But in other poems, regality acts as a foil for the speaker or the beloved. The most vehement assertion is in poem 30, in which the speaker contrasts his own vineyard with the king's, and proclaims his own to be superior. Similarly, but without the tone of defiance, the speaker of poem 20 sets his beloved against a backdrop of sixty queens, and proclaims her so remarkable that even these regal figures sing her praises. In both poems, the speaker contrasts the uniqueness of his beloved with the multitude of the regal holdings. The vineyard in poem 30 yields great wealth for its owner (the Hebrew specifies a thousand pieces of silver); in poem 20, the queens, concubines ("brides," in my translation), and young women, who are all the possessions of the king, number in the scores. But these large numbers, signifying affluence and luxury, cannot compete, in the speaker's eyes, with his one, own beloved. He would not, he declares in poem 30, trade his beloved for all of Solomon's harem.

Wealth cannot compete with love, suggest the speakers of these poems. The female speaker of poem 28 asserts even more emphatically that a man is to be scorned if he attempts to buy love in the marketplace. Even were he to offer, as the Hebrew indicates, "all the wealth of his house," he could never purchase love with money.

Wealth, however, like regality, has more than one connotation in the Song. In poem 4 the speaker offers to adorn his beloved with gold and silver, gifts offered in the spirit of love. In poem 14, the poem in which regality is most central, the splendors of wealth—gold, silver, and cedar—adorn the king's wedding procession. The exquisite appeals of the imagery—the smells of the incense, the colors of the carriage—make regality and wealth seem enthralling; as fervently as they are elsewhere scorned, they are here celebrated. This discrepancy in attitudes toward the figure of the king attests again to the benefit of reading the poems of the Song as discrete units rather than parts of a unified whole.

(f) It should by now be apparent that the Song is a text extraordinarily rich with sensory imagery. By far the most prevalent sensory material in the text is visual (especially in the *wasfs*); in addition, references to sight and to visions recur in several places (in poem 20; also in poem 17, where a flash of the beloved's eyes thrills the heart). References to smell are also abundant, as in the many mentions of flowers, fruits, spices, perfumes, and even the aroma of the Lebanon mountains. The sense of taste is evoked in several poems, always seeming to suggest erotic experience. Sound is used less metaphorically, but the sounds of voices are important erotic enticements (as in poems 9, 10, 19, and 31); and, of course, sound-plays are essential in the construction of the Hebrew verse itself, alliteration being a common poetic device. The sense of touch is evoked with every wish for the lover's embrace (for example, in the couplets preceding the adjurations in poems 8 and 25) and is further implied in some of the more elusive metaphors (breasts "like fawns" in poems 15 and 22, and like "clusters of grapes" in poem 23). Finally, synaesthesia is used to striking effect in poem 1, where a name, as remembered or heard, is associated with fragrance (see the note to poem 1 in chapter 6).

Contexts, Themes, and Motifs

While I have not treated each of the senses as a separate motif, their importance is, I hope, apparent from the discussions of the other motifs to which they relate. Indeed, there is probably nothing more essential to appreciation of poetic effect in the Song than a readiness to respond to sensuality.

CHAPTER 6

Notes to the Poems

THE FOLLOWING NOTES treat selected matters of interpretation in the individual poems; many of the comments contained here are based on discussions in the preceding chapters. Because these notes, like the rest of this study, are intended for the general reader and the Bible scholar alike, I usually direct my comments to the English poems, as presented in my translation, as well as to the Hebrew poems, as presented in my reconstruction of the original text as a lyric anthology. Citations of *lines* always refer to the lines in my translation or my reconstruction of the Hebrew; for example, line 1 of the English poem 1 is: "O for your kiss! For your love." (On occasion *chapter and verse* are referred to; these indicate the traditional divisions that appear in the Masoretic text of the Hebrew Bible.) Although the Hebrew and English poems correspond by number, the line numbers do not always correspond. For example, lines 1–2 of the Hebrew poem 3 are equivalent to line 1 of the English poem 3; line 1 of the Hebrew poem 12 is equivalent to lines 1–2 of the English poem 12.

Notes to the Poems

For readers who do not know Hebrew, word-for-word translations, which I refer to as "literal," are provided whenever the Hebrew is cited and its meaning is not apparent from the context. When alternate readings of a word or phrase are given, they are set off by commas and the word "OR" in upper case letters. Thus, in the literal translation "your name is poured, OR green, oil, " "green" is an alternate reading for "poured."

❧ TITLE

Chapter 1, verse 1, of the Hebrew, *šir haššírím ᵃšer lišlomoh,* is the wonderfully alliterative title of the work, and not part of any poem. Literally, this phrase means "the song of songs, which is by, OR to, OR of, OR about, Solomon." "The song of songs" is a superlative construction like "king of kings" or "holy of holies," and probably means "the greatest of all songs." Another interpretation is "the song composed of songs," referring to the structure of the text as a compilation. In the standard English translations, the book's title is rendered variously—"the Song of Songs," "the Song of Solo-

*Notes
to the Poems*

mon," "Canticles"—but "the Song of Songs," commonly abbreviated "the Song," is the name most used by scholars today.

The third word of the Hebrew title, *ʾᵃšer,* "which," appears nowhere else in the text; rather, the prefix *še-* is used, thirty-two times. This is evidence that the title is an editorial addition. Since the preposition preceding Solomon's name can have any of several meanings, it is unclear whether those who bestowed the title were attributing authorship of the Song to Solomon, or were dedicating the Song to him, or were claiming it to have been part of the royal possessions. The same preposition occurs with David's name in the opening lines of the Psalms, where it is probably meant to indicate that the Psalms belonged to the collection of King David, that is, were written by him. While for centuries the Song was traditionally viewed as Solomon's creation, today few, if any, scholars believe that Solomon had anything to do with the composition of the text.

Moreover, contrary to popular belief, Solomon is neither a speaker nor a principal character in the Song. His name appears in the Hebrew in six instances besides the title (poem 2, poem 14 three times, poem 30 twice), where I have sometimes rendered it as "the king." Yet in none of these poems is Solomon the speaker, and only in poem 14 is he the primary focus of attention. As explained above (chapter 5), the references to Solomon and to "the king" seem to be part of a literary motif, used to create poetic contrasts. It is unlikely that the historical person of King Solomon is intended as a persona in any of the poems.

❧ POEM 1

The opening two lines of the Hebrew have a confusing grammatical feature: the verb forms and pronominal suffixes shift from third to second person. Similarly, in lines 6 and 7 of the Hebrew, the references shift from second person back to third. Thus, KJV* translates lines 1–2, "Let *him* kiss me

---

*A key to the abbreviations that are used in this chapter appears at the back of the book.

with the kisses of *his* mouth: for *thy* love is better than wine"; and lines 6–7, "Draw me, we will run after *thee*: the King hath brought me into *his* chambers" (emphasis added, this paragraph and next). But this translation, which implies a change of characters, is misleading. In fact, the shift of grammatical person is characteristic of biblical style and should not be understood as a change of referent; so agree most commentators.[1] The assumption of a third character here violates the lyric *I-Thou* relation in the poem, and makes the causal relationship implied by the syntax—"Let him kiss me . . . *for* thy love is better than wine"—peculiar. It is better to understand the addressed beloved and the third person as the same figure. The king may be seen as a metaphor for the beloved, whose attractiveness to the speaker is described in regal (which is to say, the loftiest) terms. To emphasize this I have introduced a simile into line 6 of the English: "*Like* a king to his rooms—."

Note too that the verb in the first line of the Hebrew, *yiššaqeni*, is translated by KJV and most others as a jussive: "*let* him kiss me." The imperfect aspect (biblical Hebrew's future tense) sometimes conveys wish or command; in this poem, it expresses the mode of wishing found often in love monologues spoken by women in the Song. I rendered it here as "O for your kiss!"

The Hebrew line 4 reads, literally, "your name is poured, OR green, oil." Oil, here and throughout the Song, refers to fragrant oils used as perfumes; thus the point is that the name is sweet-smelling (hence my translation, "your . . . sweet name"). In what sense can a name be compared to a fragrance? The reference may be to the sound of the name, as suggested in the NAB translation: "Your name spoken is a spreading perfume—"; this synaesthetic interpretation suits well the erotic context. Then too, the image may have a more abstract meaning: names may be said to be like smells in their ability to mark, and thus evoke, individual identity. A sweetly fragrant name might be one that pleasantly calls to mind its bearer, much as a whiff of a familiar perfume can do. Whether as uttered or only as called to mind, the name of the beloved has powerful sensual impact on the speaker of this line. The line is further emphasized in the Hebrew by its strong semantic alliteration: *šemen turaq šᵉmekha.*[2]

❧ POEM 2

This is one of the most controversial poems in the text. Spoken by a woman to an audience of hostile observers, the city women (literally, "the daughters of Jerusalem"), it is a statement of self-affirmation and pride. Most commentators, however, read the poem, in particular the opening line, as an apology; and most translations reflect this interpretation. Virtually all standard English renditions translate the conjunction in line 1 as "but," as in KJV: "I am swarthy but comely." The exception comes only in 1989, with *The Revised English Bible*'s rendition: "I am dark and lovely." Indeed, the Hebrew conjunction *wᵉ-* means "and" far more commonly than "but"; the standard translations are based on the unfortunate assumption that blackness and beauty are contradictory.

I believe that the woman's assertion of her blackness is affirmative, not apologetic, and that the tension in the poem is the result of conflict between her and her audience. The city women stare with critical eyes, yet the speaker defies them to diminish her self-esteem. No, she argues, I will not be judged by your standards; I am black *and* I am beautiful. Thus, I read the images in the first stanza as parallel: the tents of the nomadic tribe of Kedar and the drapes of King Solomon are each dark and attractive veils. There is both pride and mystery in these images, as the speaker defies her beholders to penetrate, with their stares, the outer cloak of her skin.

The speaker knows that she is the object of public scrutiny, but she claims to be accustomed to such attention. The sun itself has gazed at her, burning her, but also, she implies, admiring her. The poem resounds with underlying paradoxes: light that causes blackness, and light that is contained in blackness—images buried in the roots of central words. The root *šzf* (in *šešᵉzafatni*) means "burn" but also "glance":

168

the eye of the heavens glances and, glancing, burns. It burns the woman "black," *šᵉḥorah,* and again "black-black," *šᵉḥar-ḥoret.* The common tendency to read *šᵉḥarḥoret* as a diminutive of *šᵉḥorah,* hence meaning "a little black" or "blackish," is counterintuitive: the doubled root suggests intensification rather than diminution. The root of these words, *šḥr,* is also the root of *šaḥar,* meaning "dawn" or, originally, "the light before the dawn." The woman is radiant in her blackness, glowing as the source of light that has burned her. Hence, "Black as the light before the dawn," in line 8 of my translation.

The last stanza presents the greatest difficulties to interpretation. It is unclear why the "mother's sons" (half-brothers? or siblings referred to by a distancing term?) are angry with the speaker, and whether her assignment as keeper of vineyards is a punishment meted out because she has neglected herself or whether the self-neglect is a result of the difficult task assigned her. In either case, the vineyards (discussed in the previous chapter of this study) are here a sexual symbol: "my own" vineyard refers to the speaker's self; the statement that she has neglected (literally, "not guarded") her own vines seems to be an allusion to her not having guarded her own sexuality. Implied is the violation of a moral norm, but it is difficult to be specific about what this norm is. I did not try to resolve all these questions of interpretation in my translation, but chose instead to let some ambiguities stand in the English as I believe they do in the Hebrew.

POEM 3

The meaning of *kᵉʿotyah* in line 4 of the Hebrew, which I translate "go searching blindly," is uncertain. KB (p. 695) suggests "wrapped, covered," and Theophile Meek reads "as one who is veiled," arguing that the veil is that of a temple prostitute.[3] KJV translates "as one that turneth aside"; RSV gives "like one who wanders." RSV's reading, which, according to Meek, is based on the emendation of the word to *kᵉṭoʿiyyah,* following the Syriac, Symmachus, and Vulgate versions,* makes most sense in context. Then again, we may be more persuaded by the reading "covered" or "veiled" if we understand it figuratively, as suggesting that the woman is blinded, unable to see her way clearly. My translation, "go searching blindly," incorporates the ideas of wandering and being unable to find one's way, and is intended to highlight the theme of searching for the beloved.

❧ POEM 4

The opening lines of the Hebrew read, literally, "to a mare in Pharaoh's chariotry / I compare you, my beloved." This image is puzzling when one realizes that only stallions, never mares, drew chariots in ancient Egypt. The meaning becomes clear only when we understand the function of mares in ancient warfare; a passage from Egyptian literature suggests that they were set loose in battle by the enemy to allure and distract the chariot-harnessed stallions of the Pharaoh: "Then, when the Prince of Kadesh sent out a mare, which [*was swift*] on her feet and which entered among the army, I ran after her on foot, carrying my *dagger*, and I (ripped) open her belly. I cut off her tail and set it before the king. Praise was given to god for it." At the word "army," the translator of the passage notes: "To stampede the stallions of the Egyptian chariotry."[4]

Thus the point of the image is not simply that the beloved is as beautiful as a regal horse, as most translations suggest, but that she is as tempting, as distracting, even as dangerous, as the presence of a single mare among many stallions.[5] Believing that this metaphor would have been clear to its original audience, I decided to make it explicit in my translation: "Like a mare among stallions." I omitted mention of Pharaoh because it would have clouded rather than illuminated the point.

---

*These versions as well as others mentioned below (Septuagint, Old Latin, Arabic, and Aquila) are ancient translations of the Bible to which scholars often refer.

In the third and fourth lines, the words *torim* and *ḥa-ruzim* are difficult. The former has uncertain meaning in context; the latter occurs only once in the Bible (a *hapax legomenon*). Most translations give "ornaments" or the like for *torim;* NJPS translates "plaited wreaths," probably because *tor*, elsewhere in the Bible and in later Hebrew, means "turn." I too read "turnings, OR plaitings" for *torim*, and see the image as referring to plaited hair ("braids" in line 3 of my translation). For *ḥaruzim,* usually taken to mean some kind of beads, I read (with KB, p. 332) "string of shells" ("shells" in line 4 of the English). Thus, as I read the poem, the woman is depicted as adorned, but with natural rather than artificial ornaments. This description of the cheeks and neck is quite appropriate to the poem's central metaphor, for, as evidenced in bas-relief depictions, the Egyptians decorated the heads and necks of their horses. The portrait of the woman that is drawn here also contrasts nicely with the images of the closing couplet, in which the speaker offers her more elaborate ornamentation: braids not of hair but of gold, studded with silver. The act of adorning the beloved with gifts is not a superfluous gilding of the lily; rather, it plays the important function of establishing the speaker's place in the love relationship.

Thus, the poem moves from a distant view of the beloved as alluring, perhaps even overwhelming, to an intimate portrait of her cheeks and neck, and finally concludes with the affirmation of *I-Thou* relation. It is a highly compressed and tightly structured lyric that achieves dramatic movement in but a few lines.

POEM 5

The difficult word in this poem is *bimsibbo* in the first line, which KJV translates "at his table," and RSV renders "on his couch." The Septuagint reads *anaklesis,* "leaning back, OR reclining," and it may be from this that RSV derives its reading. "Reclining" suggests the more private context of the bedroom with its couch for love, rather than the dining hall, so RSV's reading seems appropriate. However, I take *bimsibbo* to mean something like "in his surroundings," from the root *sbb*, "go around." The first line thus means, "Until the king is back in his surroundings," and I render it "Until the king returns." My intention was to focus in the opening line on the feelings of erotic anticipation that suffuse the poem as a whole. As in poem 1, "the king" should be understood here as a metaphorical reference to the beloved.

The specific fragrance mentioned in the Hebrew is nard, but it may be an allusion to sexual smell. There is no need to interpret the opening prepositional phrase, *'ad še-,* as referring to spatial distance. The more likely meaning "until" suggests that the woman exudes aromas in anticipation of her lover's return.

❧ POEM 6

I read the phrase *'enayikh yonim,* "your eyes [are] doves," here and in poem 15, as an ellipsis for "your eyes are like the eyes of doves." KJV reflects this interpretation with "thou hast doves' eyes," but most modern versions do not: RSV, NAB, and JB all read "your eyes are doves." Chaim Rabin observes that in Arabic literature doves were noted for their sentimental eyes; he also notes that this reading is not ungrammatical in the Hebrew.[6] My translation reflects this interpretation visually by use of the apostrophe—"your eyes / like doves' "—while leaving the heard image ambiguous, as it is in the Hebrew. (The case is somewhat different in poem 19, where the male beloved's eyes are compared to doves. The extended metaphor there makes difficult the reading "eyes like eyes of doves," and it is probable that the image in 19 is not an ellipsis.)

The imagery in the last third of this poem is of a metaphorical home outdoors. This is suggested by the adjective applied to the lovers' bed, *ra''nanah,* which today means "fresh" but biblically meant "green." The lovers' "bed" is probably a bed of leaves, as I have made explicit in lines 9–10 of the English; similarly, their "rafters" and "eaves" are images suggested by the branches of cedar and juniper trees.

The cedars of the Bible were large, broad trees (see their use as an image of grandeur in poem 19), which here spread rafterlike boughs above the lovers. Another translator who makes this interpretation explicit is James Moffatt:

> Our bed of love is the green sward,
> our roof-beams are yon cedar-boughs,
> our rafters are the firs.[7]

Lines 7–8 of the Hebrew poem, *qorot battenu ʾᵃrazim / rahiṭenu bᵉrotim* (literally, "the beams, OR rafters, of our house are cedars / our eaves are cypresses, OR junipers"), may be the speech of the two voices together or of the woman alone; the Hebrew grammar leaves this open. Although a case could be made for either reading, linguistic patterns argue for seeing these lines as part of the woman's speech. The argument is as follows: Line 6 of the Hebrew, *ʾaf ʿarśenu raʿᵃnanah* (literally, "how green is our bed"), is linked to the previous line through the repetition of the particle *ʾaf*. Line 6 is also connected to the ensuing lines 7–8, because *ʿarśenu*, "our bed," is parallel to *qorot battenu*, "the beams, OR rafters, of our house," and to *rahiṭenu*, "our eaves." Thus line 6 acts as a bridge between lines 4–5 (the woman's speech) and lines 7–8, and the final effect is that 4–8 appear to be the continuous speech of the same speaker, namely, the woman. I render 4–8 of the Hebrew as the woman's speech (English lines 7–12).

⁂ POEM 7

Like poem 4, poem 7 has a developed argument that culminates in an affirmation of *I-Thou* relation. Unlike 4, 7 is a dialogue, and the relationship here unfolds in a short sequence of statements and responses.

The key to the poem's meaning lies in the interpretation of its botanical imagery. The controversial *ḥᵃvaṣṣelet haśśaron* and *šošannat haʿᵃmaqim* of the opening stanza, translated in KJV as "rose of Sharon" and "lily of the valley," are, in the opinion of Nogah Hareuveni, the *Tulipa sharonensis* and

Narcissus tazetta.[8] While the former grows in sandy parts of
the plains and the latter in a variety of habitats, the two share
the feature of being common wildflowers. The point of the
female speaker's identification of herself with these two
flowers, then, may be that she grows, hearty as a wildflower,
in a number of locales. The male speaker responds that to
him she is unique, a singular *šošannah,* "narcissus," beside
which all other flowers seem like brambles.

She rejoins with a similar compliment, calling her beloved a fruit-bearing tree in an otherwise fruitless thicket.
The Hebrew *ya'ar,* as Hareuveni points out, could not have
meant a forest as we think of one today, but something
smaller, like a thicket, in which trees bearing edible fruit were
rarely found. In the protective shade of her lover's embrace,
the female speaker blossoms (literally, "delights"); there she
tastes the sweetness of his fruit. The specific tree mentioned
in the second stanza of the Hebrew, *tappuah,* is often mis-
translated "apple." Today we know that apples did not grow
in biblical Palestine; Hareuveni suggests instead that the *tappuah* was a quince. In poems 8, 23, and 27, I translate *tappuah*
as "quince" or "quince tree," but here, where it plays the special role of metaphor for the male beloved, I render it "sweet
fruit tree."[9]

The poem proceeds by associations, with the mutual ex-
change of praises becoming more emphatic as the dialogue
progresses, until it ends, satisfyingly, in union.

❧ POEM 8

The second line of this poem is difficult because of the word
diglo, usually taken to mean "his flag, OR banner." KJV reads
"his banner over me was love," but this is perplexing. I take
diglo to be related to the Akkadian root *dagalu,* "glance," and
read the line, literally, as "his glance upon me was love"; I
translate it "Gazing at me with love." Meek (p. 113) points
out that this root is assumed in several versions—Septuagint, Symmachus, Old Latin, Syriac, and Arabic—but they
vocalize it as an imperative: "look at me with love." I assume

the same root for two difficult words in poems 19 and 20.
Thus I read *dagul* in poem 19 as "seen," that is, visible or out-
standing among many, and render it there as "radiant" (line
25 of the English). In poem 20, I translate the difficult *nidgalot*, which appears in the third and the last lines of the Hebrew, as "visions," that is, something apprehended by sight.
This translation substitutes for the rather odd "army with
banners" offered in KJV and RSV.

The ending of poem 8 is almost identical to the endings
of poems 13 and 25: all three poems close with an adjuration
to the city women (although in the Hebrew poem 25 it is
somewhat abbreviated, the reference to the doe being omitted). I have translated the adjuration identically in all three
poems, and my translation differs substantially from the
standard versions. Literally, the last two lines are "Do not
waken, do not arouse love until it desires, OR it is satisfied."
Most versions read this as an admonition not to arouse passion prematurely; thus, RSV translates: "that you stir not up
nor awaken love until it please." But why, in the context of
these three love monologues, in which the speaker expresses
great longing to be with her lover, should she interrupt her
mood with a warning to the city women not to arouse their
own—or their lovers'—passion? KJV seems to sense this in-
congruity and translates the phrase: "that ye stir not up, nor
awaken *my love*, till *he* please" (emphasis added here and
throughout the paragraph). But this too is an awkward and
improbable reading, since nowhere else in the Song is the
male beloved referred to by the word *ha'ahʳvah*, which is
feminine in gender and means "love" in an abstract or in-
animate sense. NEB tries to solve the gender aspect of the
problem by assigning the lines to a male speaker: "Do not
rouse *her*, do not disturb *my love* until *she* is ready," but this
assignation is highly unlikely, since the oath is clearly a continuation of the female speaker's monologue in all three instances. I read this line differently from all the above
interpretations. In an attempt to keep the city women apart
from the intimate situation about which she fantasizes, the
speaker warns: "Do not rouse [that is, *do not disturb*] the *love-*

making [between the speaker and her lover] until *it* is satisfied"; hence my translation: "Not to wake or rouse us / Till
we fulfill our love."

Poems 8 and 25 also have in common the wistful couplet
"O for his arms around me, / Beneath me and above!" (literally, "his left [hand] beneath my head / and his right [hand]
embracing me"), which precedes the adjuration and which,
like it, seems formulaic. I translate this couplet as a wish ("O
for . . . ") because I believe it expresses the woman's fantasy
as she projects her situation into the future. Thus, first she
imagines the love embrace, then she warns the city women
not to disturb it. This interpretation would seem to be supported by the fact that in the only other instance where the
adjuration appears, poem 13, it follows another fantasy—of
the woman seizing and embracing her lover in the street (just
as he embraces her, in her fantasy, in poems 8 and 25). Moreover, the whole of poem 25 is clearly set in the realm of wish-
ful thinking, as we see from the poem's opening line: "Oh,
if you were my brother." The adjuration seems, in all three
instances, to express the anxiety that the speaker feels when
her lover is absent.

❧ POEM 9

"Tender grape" in line 19 of the English is a translation of
sᵉmadar (line 18 of the Hebrew), a difficult word that appears
three times in the Song and nowhere else in the Bible. In
poem 11 I render it "new grapes," and in poem 24, "tender
buds." The scholarly debate about whether *sᵉmadar* refers to
the blossom or the early fruit of the grapevine does not seem
to me crucial. As either the flower or the early fruit, it suggests tenderness and vulnerability.

Zamir (line 15 of the Hebrew), rendered "songbird" in
line 16 of the English, is another controversial word. Many
take *zamir* to mean "pruning" and *'et hazzamir* to refer to
"the pruning season" (see citations in Meek, p. 116). I find
this interpretation unlikely, since the poem is set in the
springtime, which is not the season in which to prune. The
Gezer Calendar, a Palestinian document from the tenth cen-

tury B.C.E., contains evidence that the root *zmr* refers to a summer agricultural activity, perhaps thinning of the vines, but this meaning too is out of season here.[10] Others see *zamir* as deriving from the root meaning "song" and render *'et hazzamir* as "the time of singing"; so translates RSV, while KJV specifies "the time of singing birds." Hareuveni suggests yet another possibility: the *zamir*, he believes, is the nightingale, whose mating season—that is, the time when it sings—is in the spring. Thus *'et hazzamir* refers to that time of year when the nightingale is heard. This interpretation is compatible with the poetic context not only because the season is right, but also because the phrase *'et hazzamir*, "the season of the nightingale," is in parallel position to *qol hattor*, "the sound of the turtledove." I translate the two images together as "dove and songbird singing."

❧ POEM 10

The final couplet of my English version introduces words and images not in the Hebrew. The Hebrew states, literally, "your voice [is] pleasant, your appearance [is] lovely." I render "appearance" as "body," to add concreteness. Because adjectives like *'arev*, "pleasant," and *na'weh*, "lovely" (and others found elsewhere in the Song, such as *yafeh*, "pretty, OR nice," and *tov*, "good, OR sweet"), which are frequent in biblical Hebrew, tend to fall flat in English, I have tried to render them more evocatively in the translations. Here I turned one into a simile: "Your voice clear as water." The image of water seemed right, fitting with the landscape and having appropriate metaphorical associations as well (elsewhere in the Song, in poem 18, water symbolizes the female beloved).

One might ask why it should be necessary to introduce specific images into the English if the Hebrew does well enough without them. It is difficult to say exactly how the Hebrew manages to incorporate so many "flat" adjectives without itself becoming flat verse. Perhaps one explanation is the musical quality of the original, which sustains many of the lines. For example, the repetition of Hebrew vowel patterns in the closing four lines of this poem (*har'ini 'et-mar'ayikh / hašmi'ini 'et-qolekh / ki-qolekh 'arev / umar'ekh na'weh*) adds to the effect created by the chiastic parallelism.* Because this assonance could not be easily preserved in translation, I felt that some other poetic effect was needed to compensate, and I chose, in this case, imagery.

POEM 11

Although puzzling, this poem is not opaque. As discussed in the previous chapter, the vineyards ("vines," in my translation) here symbolize female sexuality; note too that they are described as being in the vulnerable stage of *s'madar*, "early blossoming, OR new fruit." The *šu'alim* (a masculine noun), "foxes," are hostile marauders; they seem to represent male figures who are as threatening in this context as are the city guards in poem 19. As we have seen, danger lurks in the background of several poems in the Song; this one in particular seems to be a mood piece—or perhaps a fragment—emphasizing ominous undercurrents in the collection.

POEM 12

The opening two lines of the English are an expansion of the tightly compressed Hebrew line *dodi li wa'ani lo*, literally, "My lover to me and I to him." KJV, RSV, and NJPS all translate this line "My beloved is mine and I am his," indicating a passive state of possession. But the preposition *l'-*, "to," may imply something else: it may be an ellipsis for a verb of action. I read these lines not as a statement of passive possession but as an assertion of mutual, active choice; therefore, I introduce into the translation a verb suggesting physical and emotional movement: "My lover turns to me, / I turn to him." Similarly, in poem 19 I translate *'ani l'dodi*

---

*"Chiasmus" (from the Greek *chi*, X) refers to parallelisms in which certain elements of a line are reversed in a subsequent line, creating, in the most simple example, a pattern of A B / B A. In this case, the Hebrew lines, translated literally, can be analyzed as follows:

show me your *appearance* / let me hear your *voice* //
for your *voice* is pleasant / and your *appearance* is lovely.

wᵉdodi li, literally, "I to my lover and my lover to me," as "I turn to meet my love, / He'll turn to me." And in poem 24, the opening line, *ᵃni lᵉdodi wᵉᶜalay tᵉšuqato,* literally, "I to my lover and for, OR toward, OR upon, me his desire," reads, in my version, "Turning to him, who meets me with desire—." In all three of these cases, I take the preposition *lᵉ-* to imply a preceding verb of movement. These lines may have been variations on a convention, for they are remarkably similar in syntax and meaning, and I repeat the verbs "turn" and "meet" in the English poems to emphasize this similarity.

The closing line of the Hebrew, *ᶜal hare bater,* literally, "on the split, OR cut, mountains," is sometimes emended to read *ᶜal hare bᵉśamim,* literally, "on the mountains of spices," to agree with the last line of poem 31 (where I translate "on the fragrant hills").[11] Emendation is unnecessary. The image as given, *hare bater,* "split, OR cut, mountains," is a vivid geographical description, probably quite accurate. According to Hareuveni, the word *bater* refers to a geological cut and aptly describes the mountains in Galilee, which look split. On the metaphorical level, too, the image is appropriate: the female speaker banishes her beloved until nighttime, when, she hints, he can safely return to her, to play like a deer on the split mountains. I translate *ᶜal hare bater* as "in the clefts of the hills."

ও POEM 13

This poem of search-for-the-beloved exemplifies the initiative often assumed by female speakers in the Song. One is struck by the persistence of the speaker, which culminates in her unabashed declaration, "I won't let him go." Here, as in poem 25, the speaker announces her intention to bring her lover to her mother's home, where she will be free to pursue love. Also as in poem 25, this poem concludes with an adjuration to the city women not to invade the privacy of the lovemaking.

As already observed, poem 13 is in the mode of a fantasy; in fact, because the speech begins with the speaker alone in her bed, the events that follow may be viewed as part of the speaker's dream—although the dream framework is less explicit here than in poem 19, where the speaker actually declares that she is asleep. In the English version of poem 13, I tried to evoke a dreamlike atmosphere by interweaving present and future tense.

❧ POEM 14

The resonances of the opening line of the Hebrew are complex and not easily rendered in English. In biblical usage, the verb ʿolah, "rise" (which I translate "approaching, up"), has overtones of both physical and spiritual activity. It often has religious meaning, as in the sacrificial rites (literally, "offerings up") mentioned in Leviticus and elsewhere. Journeys to Jerusalem are also referred to by this verb, and in this poem, ʿolah seems to refer to such an expedition. One senses a grand, even awesome atmosphere, which colors the mood of the entire poem. I tried to recreate this mood in English by using long rhyming lines and slightly elevated diction.

"Incense," in line 2 of the English, is a descriptive rendering of mor and lᵉvonah, "myrrh" and "frankincense," in the Hebrew line 3. I avoided literal translations of these words because of their now dominant association with the Christian Nativity, which is anachronistic to the Song. In the Song, mor and lᵉvonah are primarily images of fragrance; hence, I translated them here as "incense," and elsewhere as "fragrant bloom" (penultimate stanza of poem 15) and "fragrant woods and . . . perfumes" (fourth stanza of poem 18).

The role of the mother in this poem is unique, though not incongruous with other occurrences in the Song. Elsewhere she is associated with the home and with sites for lovemaking; in poem 25, she is the one who "teaches" love. Here she plays a more formal role, crowning the king on his wedding day. Samuel Noah Kramer speculates that this passage is a late reflection of an ancient Hebrew "sacred marriage rite."[12] However, the crown need not be royal; it may refer to the headpiece worn in marriage ceremonies. As Gordis argues, "Crowns were worn even by ordinary grooms and brides, until the defeats sustained in the War against Rome in 70, when they were abandoned as a sign of mourning."[13] It is fitting that the mother, who implicitly supports the lovers' union elsewhere, sanctions it officially here.

è POEM 15

The body of this poem is a *wasf* (see chapter 4). Here I comment on the frame of the poem, that is, the lines at the beginning and toward the end, which enclose and give context to the description of the beloved's body.

The poem opens with the exclamation *hinnakh yafah ra'yati,* literally, "behold, you are fair, my beloved" ("How fine/you are, my love," in my translation), a line that duplicates the opening of poem 6. So too, lines 22–23 of the Hebrew, *'ad šeyyafuaḥ hayyom/wᵉnasu haṣṣᵉlalim,* literally, "until the day breathes/and the shadows flee" (in my translation, "Until/the day is over,/shadows gone"), are found elsewhere in the Song: in poem 12, lines 3–4 (translated, in lines 5–6 of the English, "Until the day is over/And the shadows flee"). In addition, the exclamation of the penultimate line, *kullakh yafah ra'yati,* literally, "all of you is fair, my beloved" ("How fine/you are, my love," in my translation), echoes, with somewhat more emphasis, the poem's opening line, *hinnakh yafah ra'yati.* Thus the *wasf* (which, like all *wasf*s, we may assume to be composed at least partially of conventional expressions—repeated phrases that were the common stock of oral poets) seems here also to be framed by conventional material, or at least material that appears repeatedly in the Song. Indeed, the incompleteness of this *wasf* and the duplication of part of it in poem 20 suggest that this entire poem may have been fashioned, by a poet or a compiler, from borrowed fragments and pieces. Nonetheless, the poem as we now have it stands on its own, as a well-framed love monologue praising the beloved.

è POEM 16

The verb in line 3 of the Hebrew, *tašuri,* has at least two distinct meanings: "to descend," as in Isaiah 57:9 and Ezekiel

27:25; and "to see, OR behold, OR regard," as in Numbers 23:9. Thus the third line of the Hebrew, *tašuri meroʾš ʾamanah,* may mean either "descend from the top of [Mount] Amana" or "look from the top of [Mount] Amana." KJV reads "look from the top of Amana"; RSV gives "depart from the peak of Amana" but cites "look" as an alternative for "depart." I render "come down" in the third line of the English, but incorporate both meanings in the last line, "Look down, look down and come away!" The situation of the poem, as I read it, is as follows: the woman is located in the mountaintops, the speaker somewhere in the landscape below; he calls to her, inviting her to join him, attempting to persuade her that her present habitat—aside from being intolerably far from him—is a dangerous place for her to remain.

POEM 17

The much-discussed appellation "my sister, my bride" appears twice in this poem, and twice again in poem 18. It is by now a commonplace to note that the Egyptians used "sister" as an endearing term and that the Hebrews did the same.[14] The modern reader certainly should have no difficulty reading the terms "sister" and "bride" as metaphors. Just as it is inappropriate to read "sister" literally as "sibling" here, it is unnecessary to read "bride" as significantly different from "beloved"; the poem does not seem to be about marital love any more than about a sibling relationship.

Note that in poem 25 another, this time hypothetical, reference is made to a sibling relationship. There the female speaker claims that *if* her beloved were *really* her brother, she would feel free to kiss him in public. This testifies to the social acceptability of sibling intimacy, which the speakers in poems 17 and 18 wish to evoke.

Elsewhere in the Song, as in poems 2 and 29, sibling relationships are depicted as real rather than as either metaphorical or hypothetical; in these cases, they are fraught with conflict. There is no contradiction here; indeed, it is quite understandable that real familial relations are portrayed as less ideal than hypothetical or metaphorical ones. The darker undercurrents of poems 2 and 29 need not complicate our understanding of the references in 17, 18, and 25.

❧ POEM 18

Coming at almost the midpoint of the text is the archetypal "garden poem," in which the extended metaphor of the garden—which has come to represent ideal love in the Western tradition—governs from beginning to end.[15] The garden here functions dually: as context—the setting where the lovers meet—and as metaphor for the beloved. The speaker addresses his beloved as a garden; she replies by referring to "my garden" (myself, my sexuality), which then becomes, in her words in the Hebrew, "his garden"; finally *he* speaks of "*my* garden," entering at once into both the physical context and the love relationship.

The garden is described as lush with flowers, spices, and fruits, and eating and drinking are central erotic motifs. Images of water are also central: the garden as metaphor for the female beloved parallels the pool and the fountain in the opening lines. Later, the beloved is referred to as a fountain, a well of living water, flowing streams. While water seems to be the substance that nurtures all the plants *in* the garden, as another metaphor for the beloved it is also *equivalent to* the garden.

One cannot unravel the interwoven layers of meaning in the poem without rending the fabric of the whole. The garden metaphor depends on a special kind of logic, appropriate to the paradoxes of the love relationship. Because I am nourished by my beloved, implies the male speaker, my beloved is my garden. But since she possesses the particular pleasurable and sensual qualities of water, flowers, fruits, and spices, she is also, at various times and in various ways, each thing *in* the garden. Thus she herself is located *in* the garden, and I enter the symbolic garden on both levels. I am *with* her, inside the place she inhabits, and *in* her, inside her self. And thus I experience the ultimate paradox of union in love, of two distinct selves joining together and yet remaining two.

It follows from this reading that the closing exclamation of the poem (rendered in my translation, "Feast, drink—and drink deeply—lovers!") is spoken *to* the lovers by those outside the love relationship. To read the line otherwise—as an invitation to other friends, spoken by one or both of the lovers—violates rather grotesquely the metaphor of the garden as an enclosed and intimate world.

❧ POEM 19

Because this poem is so much longer and structurally more complex than the others in the collection, it has been treated extensively in the preceding chapters. Here I add comments on two idiomatic Hebrew phrases.

Line 12 of the Hebrew, *ume'ay hamu 'alaw*, is, literally, "and my bowels churned, OR rumbled, for him." Phyllis Trible suggests that *me'ay* means "womb,"[16] but the usual reading of the line is more figurative: for the ancient Hebrews, the bowels were the seat of the emotions. The equivalent in English literary convention is the heart; hence my translation, "and my heart leaps for him!" (line 10 of the English).

Line 19 of the Hebrew, *nafši yaṣ'ah b'dabb'ro*, literally, "my soul went out upon his speaking, OR with his words" (rendered, in line 16 of my translation, as "I run out after him"), is difficult. Meek (p. 128) suggests "My soul went forth upon his speaking" or "upon his turning away," and interprets this to mean, "I fainted when he spoke" or "I fainted when he turned away." But there is a simpler interpretation: as the narrative is recorded in a dream state, the "soul" may be a figure for the self, and "his speaking" a figure for the beloved; thus, "*I* run out after *him*." Note too that the actions that ensue are searching (*biqqaštihu*) and calling out (*q'ra'tiw*). It seems unlikely that the speaker would rush into such activity immediately upon fainting. It is better to read the difficult idiom *nafši yaṣ'ah b'dabb'ro* as the beginning of a single extended—and urgent, even frenzied—pursuit of the beloved. To convey this, I have compressed lines 19–21 of the Hebrew, *nafši yaṣ'ah b'dabb'ro/ biqqaštihu w'lo' m'ṣa'tihu/q'ra'tiw w'lo' 'anani* (literally, "my soul went out upon his speaking / I searched for him and did not find him / I called to him and he did not answer me") into the English lines: "I run out after him, calling, / but he is gone."

࠸ POEM 20

This poem appears to be a string of fragments, and one might maintain that it is not a coherent poetic unit. I would argue, however, that these fragments, which I treat as four stanzas, accrue resonance from each other, together forming a powerful statement of praise for the beloved. The motif of seeing, which recurs in each of the stanzas, effectively links the stanzas together and suggests that they constitute a single poetic whole.

The poem opens with an exclamation of awe at the sight of the beloved, who is compared to two capital cities: Tirza, in the northern kingdom, and Jerusalem, in Judea. A difficult word in this first stanza is *nidgalot*, a form appearing twice in this poem but nowhere else in the Bible, and usually translated "army with banners," from the root *dgl*, meaning "flag." This reading makes little sense in context; it is better to read *nidgalot* as "visions," from the Akkadian *dagalu*, meaning "glance" (compare *diglo* in poem 8 and *dagul* in poem 19, discussed in the note to poem 8). Gordis (pp. 90–92) also argues for this reading of *nidgalot*, accounting for the feminine plural suffix of the word in the first stanza by reference to the cities of Tirza and Jerusalem, and in the fourth stanza by reference to the heavenly bodies. The first stanza ends with the speaker's admonition to his beloved to avert her eyes, for her gaze makes him tremble.

The second stanza is a fragment of the *wasf* found in poem 15. Referring back to 15, from which these lines are repeated almost exactly, we see that there the preceding image was of the beloved's eyes. Similarly, here the image of eyes at the end of the first stanza leads into the descriptions of hair, teeth, and forehead, which constitute the second stanza.

In the third stanza, the beloved is highlighted against a context of queens, concubines ("brides," in my translation), and young women. She alone stands out, as unique as the "narcissus in the brambles" of poem 7. To the speaker she is as singular as an only child (the Hebrew says, literally, "one is she to her mother/pure is she to the one who bore her"). So does she appear to the young women as well, who praise her upon seeing her beauty.

The word *barah,* "pure," links the third and fourth stanzas, and we see from the fourth stanza that the connotations of this word, too, are visual. An alternate meaning of *barah* is "bright"; I tried to preserve this sense by using "bright" for the translation of *yafah* (literally, "pretty, OR nice") in the preceding parallel line. The woman herself appears as a cosmic figure, staring down from the heavens, bright as the moon and pure-bright as the sun. *Šahar,* literally, "dawn," may refer to the morning star, Venus, or, more likely, the sun itself (note the association with the sun in poem 2); I translate it "dawn's eye." Here, as in poem 2, celestial globes are depicted as staring eyes, and the motif of vision is thus sustained through the last stanza.

There is a bold and primal quality to this final stanza. The words for moon and sun are not the usual *yareah* and *šemeš,* but the more vivid *l'vanah,* whose root means "white," and *hamah,* whose root means "hot." I make these associations explicit in the translations "white moon" and "hot sun." The awesome tone here harks back to the mood of the opening stanza; both stanzas close with the striking *nidgalot,* "visions." The appearance of this unusual word twice in one poem now seems highly purposeful: more than an inclusion (a rhetorical device that provides an outer poetic frame), *nidgalot* pulls together the internal motif of seeing that has recurred in various ways within the poem. If the four stanzas of this poem were not originally composed to form a unit, they were no doubt strung together by a very skillful compiler. The poem as it stands conveys the thrill of gazing upon the beloved, whose own glance is as powerful as the sun's.

❧ POEM 21

The phrase "the signs of spring" (line 2 of the English) is an interpretation of *'ibbe hannahal,* literally, "fruits of the valley,

OR of the riverbed." Hareuveni suggests that *'ibbe* may refer to reeds, *'ibbuvim*, which, like walnut trees, grow near streams. The reeds appear in the spring season, at the time of the flowering of the vines and pomegranate trees. The word *'ibbe* may also be related to *'aviv*, a springtime month or the first stage of ripening.

Chapter 6, verse 12, of the Hebrew, which is set apart from poem 21 (at the bottom of the page) in my reconstruction of the Hebrew text, is the only line in the Song that I have not rendered in English. I find it impossible even to offer a literal translation of this singularly garbled line; almost everyone agrees that, as it stands, it is unintelligible. Meek (p. 134) states flatly, "This is the one hopelessly corrupt verse in the Song," and the standard translations would seem to confirm this view. KJV reads: "Or ever I was aware, my soul made me like the chariots of Ammi-nadib"; without much improvement, RSV offers: "Before I was aware, my fancy set me in a chariot beside my prince." Individual scholars have made some ingenious attempts to render sense out of ostensible nonsense here, but so much emendation is involved in their efforts that few of the original words remain intact. For example, Gordis (p. 67), basing his interpretation in part on an emendation proposed by Naphtali Tur-Sinai, translates this verse, "I am beside myself with joy,/For there wilt thou give me thy myrrh,/O noble kinsman's daughter!"[17] I agree with Meek (p. 134) that "any restoration is a guess, and although many have been offered there is none that is satisfactory"; it seems that even when the Hebrew line is emended to have some syntactic coherence, it still makes little semantic sense in its poetic context. Admitting defeat, I omit this line from my translation. [18]

❧ POEM 22

This poem, the Song's only complete *wasf* describing a female figure, is studded with controversial words, phrases, and expressions. Its most difficult images are those of natural and architectural phenomena set in particular places. We are given, in the Hebrew, eyes like pools in Heshbon, at the gates of Bat-Rabbim; a nose (or, as I interpret it, face) like the tower of Lebanon overlooking Damascus; a head like Mount Carmel. Heshbon was a city located east of the Dead Sea; Damascus was, as now, the capital of Syria; Carmel was and is a mountain on the Mediterranean coast, north of present-day Haifa. Because these names no longer carry the resonance they once did, I omit them from the translation and refer instead to their visual associations. Thus the eyes are like pools, languid and reflective; the face is a tower that surveys its surroundings; the head has a commanding height, a majestic quality that is carried through in the regal imagery of the poem's last two lines.

The word *'appekh,* which I translate "your face," is rendered "your nose" in most other versions, producing the much-discussed image of a towering nose. There are a number of reasons to read *'appekh* as "your face" here, beginning with the fact that *'af* seems to mean "face" in other biblical passages, for example Genesis 3:19. More to the point at hand, the parts of the anatomy described in this passage, as in the other complete *wasf* in poem 19, are in a linear progression, in this case from bottom to top. There is, in fact, a strict adherence here to order: none of the parts is out of place. It follows, then, that after the description of the eyes and before the reference to the whole head, we are given a description not of the nose but rather of the general appearance of the face. Moreover, a face may be described by the adjective that follows here, *sofeh,* "scouting, OR looking out" ("overlooking," in my translation)—but this description is quite unfitting for a nose. Finally, the neck in this *wasf* is also described as being like a tower; a towerlike neck implies length and grandeur, but a towerlike nose seems especially ridiculous following so closely on the description of the neck. Are the neck and the nose to be seen as similar in stature or size? Surely not. Rather, the image of the face is a natural continuation of the image of the neck: as the neck is long and stately, the face is elevated and looks forth from its height. The sense of elevation or grandeur is then consummated by the description of the head and hair: mountainlike, majestic, able to capture a king.

The word *šor°rekh*, usually translated "your navel," is also difficult. It probably refers to the vulva, coming as it does in sequence after the description of the thighs and before the belly; according to Meek (p. 135), the Arabic cognate suggests this reading. I rendered the word as "hips," in hopes that the conjunction with "bowl of nectar" makes the eroticism clear.

The word *šulammit* in the first line of the Hebrew, usually given in English as a transliterated proper name, "Shulammite," is controversial. Some suggest that it derives from the name Solomon (so Meek, pp. 134–35); others emend to Shunammite, woman of Shunem, the domicile of Abishag (I Kings 1:3).[19] None of the various scholarly proposals seems to me convincing. I chose not to muddle the English poem with an enigmatic proper name, and instead translated the word as "princess," taking my cue from *bat-nadiv*, "daughter of nobility," another appellation for the woman given a few lines later in the Hebrew. As the poem culminates with regal imagery, it is likely that regality is suggested at the outset.

Finally, the dance referred to in this poem has a curious Hebrew name: *m°ḥolat hammaḥ°nayim*. It may be the dance of a particular place, *maḥ°nayim*, mentioned in Genesis 32:3; or it may be understood as "dance of two camps," from *ma-ḥ°neh*, "camp." RSV renders "dance before two armies." Although the exact meaning of the phrase is uncertain, it seems to refer to a performance before a group of people, and the description that follows leads one to think of belly dancing, probably in the nude.

❧ POEM 23

"Clusters of dates" in line 4 of the English is a translation of *'aškolot*, literally, "clusters," in line 4 of the Hebrew. KJV assumes "clusters of grapes," but this is incongruous with the figure of the palm tree. Furthermore, in line 7 the Hebrew specifies *'ešk°lot haggefen*, "clusters of the vine," for a purposeful shift of imagery. It is at this point that the portrait changes from that of a stately palm tree to a free-flowing se-

quence of disconnected images, parts of imagined experience: your breasts will be like clusters of the vine, that is,
tender as grapes; your breath will be like quinces, that is, fragrant; your palate [will taste] like wine.

The closing lines of the Hebrew poem, *wᵉḥikkekh kᵉyeyn
haṭṭov / holekh lᵉdodi lᵉmeyšarim / dovev śifte yᵉšenim,* are among
the most difficult in the Song. Literally, they are "your palate
is like good wine / going to my beloved [masculine]
smoothly, OR like new wine, / gliding over, OR stirring, the
lips of sleepers." *Lᵉmeyšarim,* "smoothly, OR like new wine,"
is a difficult form; *dovev,* "gliding, OR stirring," is a *hapax legomenon. Dodi,* the term for the male beloved in the Song, is
out of place here because a man is speaking to a woman, and
it is therefore emended by many to *dodim,* "lovers"; alternatively, NEB reads *doday,* "my caresses." *Śifte yᵉšenim,* "lips of
sleepers," makes little sense and is emended by the Septuagint, Aquila, and Syriac to "my lips and teeth"; the Vulgate
gives "his lips and teeth"; others read "lips and teeth" (as
cited by Meek, p. 39). NAB and NEB follow the last emendation and translate "lips and teeth." None of the proposed
emendations for these difficult words and phrases helps the
sense much, and even after emendation it remains impossible
to find a coherent literal reading of these lines. Hence, my
translation is a free reworking of the ideas and images suggested by the Hebrew: "And your mouth will awaken / All
sleeping desire / Like wine that entices / The lips of new
lovers."

❧ POEM 24

For discussion of the opening line, see the note to poem 12.

Kᵉfarim, in line 3 of the Hebrew, is usually translated
"villages," but it can also be the plural form of *kofer,* meaning
"henna." *Kofer,* which appears also in the Hebrew poem 5,
line 5, (translated as "blossoms," in line 7 of the English
poem), fits perfectly with the flowering environment here;
hence my translation of *kᵉfarim* as "henna" (line 3 of the English). NJPS renders *kᵉfarim* here as "henna shrubs."

The movement of "returning" (line 9 of my translation) is not explicit in the Hebrew but is suggested by the shift of contexts from the countryside to the home, and by the implied passage of time.

≈ POEM 25

T^{e}lamm^{e}deni (line 7 of the Hebrew, line 6 of the English) can mean either "she teaches me" or "you [masculine] teach me." I read the former, with the third-person pronoun referring to "my mother."

The closing adjuration of the Hebrew poem is an abbreviated and slightly altered form of the adjuration that appears in poems 8 and 13. There is, however, some weak textual evidence for the complete adjuration here in four Hebrew manuscripts and the Greek and Arabic versions.[20] Mainly to emphasize the similarities in the three poems where the adjuration occurs (8, 13, and 25), and to call attention to its formulaic nature, I have translated it identically each time.

≈ POEM 26

This poem seems to be a fragment, the first line of the Hebrew (rendered as two lines in the English) being a duplication of the opening line of the Hebrew poem 14. While poem 26 constitutes but half of a biblical verse, it is thematically distinct from the second half of that verse, and I saw no reason to join them.

≈ POEM 27

This short three-line poem in Hebrew is the second half of the biblical verse from which poem 26 is fashioned. Yet unlike poem 26, poem 27 stands on its own quite satisfactorily. While many commentators assume that a man speaks here, it is a masculine singular "you" that is addressed, strongly indicating a female speaker.

The word *ḥibbⁱlatᵉkha*, which I translate "conceived," is a verbal form of the root *ḥbl*, which sometimes refers to the labor of childbirth. Thus KJV translates: "there thy mother brought thee forth." In Psalms 7:15, however, *yᵉḥabbel* (another verbal form of the same root) is the first in a sequence of three verbs, the others being *harah*, "be pregnant," and *yalad*, "give birth"; the order suggests that *yᵉḥabbel* means "conceive" rather than "bear." Supporting this reading, the Syriac cognate of this verb can also mean either "to conceive" or "to bear" (see KB, p. 271). "Conceive" best fits the situation of poem 27; the speaker indicates that the place where she arouses her beloved is also the place where his mother has made love. As we have seen in other poems, the outdoor country setting is conducive to lovemaking, and the figure of the mother supports erotic atmosphere; thus, the speaker refers to the sexual experience of her lover's mother as erotic stimulation. The mention of labor pains would hardly seem to have the same effect.

➋ POEM 28

The tone of this Hebrew poem is unlike that of any other in the collection. The strong parallelisms, the extensive use of alliteration, and the sweeping images of fire and water all contribute to the dramatic mood. As with poem 27 some commentators assume a male speaker here, but the pronominal suffixes indicate that a male is being addressed, making a female speaker likely.

The opening lines are, literally, "put me like a seal on your heart / like a seal on your arm," and are often understood as a reference to amulets worn on the chest or arm. The seal may have been a sign of ownership (as in Genesis 38:18), but this meaning, as we shall see, is inappropriate here and is directly negated by the poem's ending. In keeping with the fiery imagery of the poem, I have suggested in my translation the stronger image of an emblem pressed or seared into the flesh. So too the *Zohar*, the central work of Kabbalah, comments: "'Set me as a seal upon thy heart.' For, as the imprint of the seal is to be discerned even after the seal is with-

The word *šalhevetyah,* which I translate "a fierce/and holy blaze," contains the emphatic particle suffix, *-yah,* which has traditionally been viewed as a reference to the name of God, the only such reference in the Song. Most translations render this word without mentioning God, as in "a most vehement flame" (KJV and RSV) and "a blazing flame" (NJPS). Meek (p. 144) suggests "flame of Yah," finding the meaning "emphatic in accordance with the Hebrew idiom of using the divine name with superlative force." I have deliberately retained just a hint of the word's sacral association in my translation, "holy blaze."

Indeed, the poem has cosmic, if not religious, overtones. *Mayim rabbim* (line 7), literally, "many, OR great, waters," which I translate "Endless seas and floods,/Torrents" (lines 9–10 of the English), may be a reference to a mythical force, the waters of chaos.²² *Š^e'ol* (line 4), which I translate (with KJV and RSV) "the grave" (line 6 of the English), is actually the place of the dead in Hebrew cosmology. While "the grave" may seem a weak equivalent for *š^e'ol,* the alternatives are worse; "hell," for example, has many inappropriate connotations, and could not be used.

The poem closes with an aphorism, leading from the world of myth into the realm of human mores and behavior. The message of the poem is emphatic: love cannot be bought, and those who try to acquire love with money will be scorned, or will find their offer met with scorn (the Hebrew pronoun *lo,* indicating the object of the reprobation, may refer either to the buyer or to his wealth). It is clear now that the "seal" of the opening lines is not a sign of acquired possession, since the poem argues vehemently against viewing love as an object that can be owned.

Thus, mythic vision climaxes in didactic pronouncement, giving the poem a sermonic shape. Yet the poem remains, first and essentially, a love lyric, which opens with an entreaty to the beloved; it should not be reduced to the moral lesson of its closing adage. Perhaps to avoid this risk,

JB isolates the last stanza and labels it an appendix, the "Aphorism of a Sage." But this cuts off the resolution of the speech and denies poetic closure. Rather, the poem should be seen as a complex unit that moves from an intense personal plea to a cosmic statement, and finally closes with a pronouncement of practical morality.

❧ POEM 29

This dialogue is one of the more enigmatic poems in the collection. To begin with, it is difficult to say who is speaking, and to whom. The opening voice sounds like a chorus of older brothers (like, perhaps, the men who sent their sister out to tend vines in poem 2), but from a purely grammatical standpoint it could represent a group of men, or women, or both. Another possibility is that the first stanza is spoken by the woman's brothers, and the second by her suitors. I find this unlikely, however, and read both stanzas as the speech of the woman's brothers, to whom she replies in the third stanza.

The imagery, too, is strange. The Hebrew states baldly that the little sister "has no breasts"; I render this more softly: "We have a young sister/Whose breasts are but flowers." "If she's a wall," the speakers say, they will build her a parapet of silver; however, "if she's a door," they will board her up with cedar. Besides describing the sister's adolescent physique, the wall and door have other levels of symbolic meaning, the impenetrable surface of the wall suggesting chastity and the door implying the opposite. Thus, silver is the reward given to the woman for having kept herself chaste, while the plank of cedar that boards her up is her punishment if she has been wanton. This interpretation sees the young woman's brothers as protective to the point of being punitive, much like the brothers referred to in poem 2.

Another reading, which I find less likely, is that the wall and the door are more synonymous, both merely architectural images. The brothers offer to adorn their sister with

precious commodities, silver and cedar, to make her more attractive to potential suitors.

Whichever way we read the brothers' speech, the sister's
reply remains adamant. She rejects their offer, stating
proudly that her breasts are "towers," fully developed, in her
own estimation. She needs no assistance from these men, for
she has already found peace with her lover.

The meaning of the unusual phrase *moṣ'et šalom,* "find
peace," is no doubt similar to that of the more common
moṣe't ḥen, "find favor." The speaker indicates that she has
found favor in her lover's eyes and, therefore, in her own. Although the expression "find peace" may seem less than idiomatic, it is consonant with the central imagery of the
poem: built on the conceit of war, the poem concludes, fit-
tingly, with a truce. In the battle with her brothers, the
young woman emerges triumphant. Because she is her own
fortress, she needs no defenders, and can establish peace on
her own terms.[23]

❧ POEM 30

This poem, too, is difficult. The grammar does not specify
the speaker's gender; this determination depends largely on
how one reads the symbol of the vineyard. In poem 2, the
vineyard represents the woman's sexuality; there, a woman
refers to her "own" vineyard, that is, to an aspect of herself.
If a similar reading applies here, one might argue that the
speaker of this poem is also a woman. But King Solomon is
said, in this poem, to own a vineyard; if the vineyard symbolizes the female *self,* this statement would nonsensically
imply that King Solomon *is* a female. It is better to read the
vineyard here as a symbol for the female *other* rather than the
female *self,* from which we can deduce that the speaker, like
King Solomon, is a man—and that both these men lay claim
to female "others." Woman as sexual "other," then, may be
treated as a beloved (the speaker's relationship to his "own"
vineyard) or as a sexual object (Solomon's vineyard is a
harem that must be kept under constant guard). Using the

motif of regality as foil, the poem advocates *I-Thou* relation and rejects the debasement of sexuality inherent in treating others as sexual objects or property.

❧ POEM 31

With this final poem we return to the garden and the world of the two lovers. Once again the theme of secret love emerges: the woman chases her beloved away lest they be caught by day, implying an invitation to return to her later, at night. A false closure is suggested in this banishment; the poem and thus the collection conclude, in fact, on a note of anticipation. If we see the Song of Songs as a collection of lyrics—that is, a string of separate moments rather than a unified structure with beginning, middle, and end—we may find it particularly fitting that it closes in expectation of the moment to come.

Key to Abbreviations

The following abbreviations appear in chapter 6 of the translator's study:

JB   *The Jerusalem Bible* (1966)

KB   Koehler and Baumgartner, *Lexicon in Veteris Testamenti Libros* (1958)

KJV   *The Holy Bible* (Authorized or King James Version, 1611)

NAB   *The New American Bible* (1970)

NEB   *The New English Bible* (1970)

NJPS   *Tanakh: The Holy Scriptures* (new Jewish Publication Society translation, 1985)

RSV   *The Holy Bible* (Revised Standard Version, 1952)

Endnotes

➶ CHAPTER 1: *Translation as a Journey*

1. Martin Buber, "The Life of the Hasidim," in *Hasidism and Modern Man*, trans. Maurice Friedman (New York: Harper & Row, 1966), p. 102.

2. In subsequent chapters, I use the words "literal" and "literally" to refer to word-for-word translations of isolated words, phrases, and lines, intended to be as exact as possible. These are offered mainly to explain points about the original to the reader who does not know Hebrew and to clarify specific departures in various translations, primarily my own.

3. I am indebted to Leo Spitzer for his notion of the "to-and-fro voyage" in literary interpretation, which I have extended by analogy. Spitzer speaks of the "voyage from certain outward details to the inner center and back again to other details" as the process by which we come to know a text. See "Linguistics and Literary History," in *Linguistics and Literary History: Essays in Stylistics* (Princeton: Princeton University Press, 1948), pp. 19–20.

4. Although Hebrew has been revived as a living spoken language in our century, the contemporary idiom is significantly different from the ancient tongue.

5. Preface to *The Holy Bible: Revised Standard Version* (New York: Thomas Nelson, 1946–1952), pp. iii–iv.

6. For knowledge of the aims and principles behind the Buber-Rosenzweig translation, I am indebted to the work of Everett Fox, much of which he shared with me in correspondence and conversation. Fox's doctoral dissertation, "Technical Aspects of the Translation of Genesis of Martin Buber and Franz Rosenzweig" (Dept. of Near Eastern and Judaic Studies, Brandeis University, 1974), provides otherwise unavailable exegesis and background of this text. See also Fox's own Bible translations, modeled after the work of Buber and Rosenzweig: *In the Beginning: A New English Rendition of the Book of Genesis* (New York: Schocken Books, 1983), first published as *In the Beginning: An English Rendition of the Book of Genesis* (*Response*, no. 14 [Summer 1972]: 1–159); and *Now These Are the Names: A New English Rendition of the Book of Exodus* (New York: Schocken Books, 1986).

7. Martin Buber, "Ueber die Wortwahl in einer Verdeutschung der Schrift" (1930), in Martin Buber and Franz Rosen-

zweig, *Die Schrift und ihre Verdeutschung* (Berlin: Schocken Verlag, 1936), pp. 135–37. The English translation of this quotation is from Fox, *In the Beginning* (1972), Translator's Afterword, p. 146.

8. Nahum Glatzer, Introduction to Fox, *In the Beginning* (1972), p. 5.

9. This and subsequent quotations from Scholem's text are from "At the Completion of Buber's Translation of the Bible," trans. Michael A. Meyer, in *The Messianic Idea in Judaism and Other Essays on Jewish Spirituality*, (New York: Schocken Books, 1971), pp. 314–19.

10. Two of the five volumes of Fox's Torah are completed (see endnote 6, above).

෴ CHAPTER 2: *The Literary Structure of the Song of Songs*

1. H. H. Rowley, "The Interpretation of the Song of Songs," in *The Servant of the Lord and Other Essays on the Old Testament*, 2d ed. (Oxford: Basil Blackwell, 1965), pp. 197–245.

2. Marvin H. Pope, *The Song of Songs: A New Translation with Introduction and Commentary* (New York: Doubleday, 1977), pp. 34–37, 40–54, 89–229.

3. Idiosyncratically, Pope concludes his survey with several pages on funeral rites, a relatively unexplored area that he believes is "capable of explaining the Canticles better than any other and is able to subsume aspects of other modes of interpretation as enfolding elements of truth" (ibid., p. 229).

4. A typical example is Leroy Waterman, *The Song of Songs: Translated and Interpreted as a Dramatic Poem* (Ann Arbor: University of Michigan Press, 1948). Among other things, Waterman transposes 3:6–4:6 to follow 1:1 in order to make his theory of the plot fit the text.

5. J. Cheryl Exum, "A Literary and Structural Analysis of the Song of Songs," *Zeitschrift für die alttestamentliche Wissenschaft* 85 (1973): 47–79. All quotations from Exum in this chapter are from this article. Other recent attempts to demonstrate structural unity in the Song are found in Francis Landy, "Beauty and the Enigma: An Inquiry into Some Interrelated Episodes of the Song of Songs," *Journal for the Study of the Old Testament* 17 (1980): 55–106; Williams H. Shea, "The Chiastic Structure of the Song of Songs," *Zeitschrift für die alttestamentliche Wissenschaft* 92 (1980): 378–96; and Edwin C. Webster, "Pattern in the Song of Songs," *Journal for the Study of the Old Testament* 22 (1982): 73–93. Landy expands upon his argument in his book *Paradoxes of Paradise: Identity and Difference in the Song of Songs* (Sheffield, Eng.: Almond Press, 1983). Michael V. Fox, in his comparative study *The Song of Songs and the Ancient Egyptian Love Songs* (Madison: University of Wisconsin Press, 1985), main-

tains that the Song is "an artistic unity." And Phyllis Trible offers a fascinating analysis of the Song "in five major movements of varying lengths" as part of a larger feminist reading of its themes and motifs in *God and the Rhetoric of Sexuality* (Philadelphia: Fortress Press, 1978), chap. 5.

6. For analyses of the features of biblical poetry that relate to oral composition, see Perry Yoder, "A-B Pairs and Oral Composition in Hebrew Poetry," *Vetus Testamentum* 21 (1971): 470–89; and Robert C. Culley, *Oral Formulaic Language in the Biblical Psalms* (Toronto: University of Toronto Press, 1967).

7. Franz Landsberger, "Poetic Units Within the Song of Songs," *Journal of Biblical Literature* 73 (1954): 204. Landsberger calls this phenomenon "juxtaposition of key words," where "key word" is equivalent to the term "catchword" as it is employed in studies of oral literature.

8. The exception might be James L. Kugel, who, in his insightful but controversial book *The Idea of Biblical Poetry: Parallelism and Its History* (New Haven: Yale University Press, 1981), calls into question the appropriateness of a binary distinction between biblical poetry and prose.

9. See Robert H. Pfeiffer, *Introduction to the Old Testament*, 2d ed. (New York: Harper, 1948), pp. 708ff., where a partial list of those in accord with the view of the Song as a collection is given. This is Pfeiffer's own view as well. See also Landsberger, "Poetic Units," p. 203, where some more recent exponents of this position are cited. Landsberger states his concurrence with those "who see in the Song of Songs, as it is extant, not a connected whole but a collection of several poems." Roland Murphy, "Towards a Commentary on the Song of Songs," *Catholic Biblical Quarterly* 39 (1977): 482–96, has argued that "the Song is a collection of love poems that have been given a certain unity by means of a dialogue pattern, and by the use of catchwords and repetitions." Murphy notes that the view of the Song as a collection "seems to be growing." Pope (*The Song of Songs*, pp. 40–54) cites several proponents of this view in his summary of the debate over structural unity, which he concludes thus: "The present writer . . . has not been convinced by any of the efforts to demonstrate or restore order or logical progression."

10. Robert Gordis, *The Song of Songs: A Study, Modern Translation, and Commentary* (New York: Jewish Theological Seminary of America, 1961), pp. 16–17. Further quotations from Gordis in this chapter are from pp. 17–18 of his book.

11. This is an example of the principle of "juxtaposition of key words," referred to above by Landsberger. In a similar application of this principle, Landsberger separates 1:5 from 1:6, arguing that

Endnotes   these are two distinct poems juxtaposed because the word "black" appears in both. I treat 1:5–6 as a single poem.

  ❧ CHAPTER 3: *Types of Love Lyrics in the Song of Songs*

    1. Martin Buber, *I and Thou*, trans. Walter Kaufmann (New York: Scribner, 1970), pp. 53–85.

    2. Throughout this study, I use the word "beloved" to refer to the loved one, as opposed to "lover," which designates the speaker or initiator. Obviously, women and men can play either role in the poems—and do.

    3. This is not apparent in the English version of poem 1 where, to avoid confusion, I changed the third-person pronoun to the second person. See the note to poem 1 in chapter 6 for further explanation.

    4. The word *wᵉyihᵉyu-na'* (line 7 of the Hebrew) grammatically indicates this mode through the particle suffix *-na'*, which implies a wish.

    5. Shelomo Dov Goitein, *'Omanut hassippur bammiqra'* (The art of the biblical story) (Jerusalem: Jewish Agency Aliyah and Youth Division, 1957), p. 106.

    6. Chaim Rabin, "The Song of Songs and Tamil Poetry," *Studies in Religion* 3 (1973–74): 205–19.

    7. Carol Meyers, "Gender Imagery in the Song of Songs," *Hebrew Annual Review* 10 (1986): 218.

    8. Other scholars have noted the absence of domination in the Song. For example, Phyllis Bird: "[The Song of Song's] power and beauty are expressed in a relationship of complete mutuality, controlled neither by the man nor by the woman" ("Images of Women in the Old Testament," in *Religion and Sexism*, ed. Rosemary Radford Ruether [New York: Simon & Schuster, 1974], p. 82); and Phyllis Trible: "Neither male nor female asserts power or possession over the other. . . . [In the Song of Songs] there is no male dominance, no female subordination, and no stereotyping of either sex" (*God and the Rhetoric of Sexuality* [Philadelphia: Fortress Press, 1978], pp. 159–61).

  ❧ CHAPTER 4: *The Waṣf*

    1. Richard N. Soulen, "The *Waṣfs* of the Song of Songs and Hermeneutic," *Journal of Biblical Literature* 86 (1967): 185.

    2. M. H. Segal, "The Song of Songs," *Vetus Testamentum* 12 (1962): 480.

    3. Waterman, *The Song of Songs*, p. 63.

4. "Potato" by Shinkichi Takahashi, trans. Harold P. Wright, in Robert Bly, *Leaping Poetry: An Idea with Poems and Translations* (Boston: Beacon Press, 1975), p. 19.

5. Bly, *Leaping Poetry*, p. 4.

6. This remark and all subsequent quotations from Soulen are from "The *Wasfs*," pp. 183–90.

7. Goitein, *'Omanut hassippur bammiqra'*, p. 106.

8. Shelomo Dov Goitein, "Našim k'yosrot suge sifrut bam-miqra'" (Women as creators of types of literature in the Bible), in *'Iyyunim bammiqra'* (Bible studies) (Tel Aviv: Yavneh, 1967), pp. 248–317.

9. By 1985 one finds new assumptions embedded in the writings of scholars who make no particular claim to a feminist perspective: "Nor do we detract from the creative genius of the Song's author in recognizing that *she or he* was heir to the resources of a long tradition" (M. Fox, *The Song of Songs and the Ancient Egyptian Love Songs*, p. xxvii; emphasis mine).

10. For this and other observations relevant to the relationship between folk culture and female tradition as reflected in the Song, again see Meyers's incisive essay "Gender Imagery in the Song of Songs," pp. 209–23. Also see Meyers, *Discovering Eve: Ancient Israelite Women in Context* (New York: Oxford University Press, 1988).

11. Fortunately, the critical voices are changing today as feminist interpretation of the Song gains more widespread acceptance. For example, the work of feminist Bible scholar Phyllis Trible, which eloquently demonstrates the absence of sexism in the Song ("Depatriarchalizing in Biblical Interpretation," *Journal of the American Academy of Religion* 41 [1973]: 30–48; reprinted in Trible, *God and the Rhetoric of Sexuality*, pp. 144–65), has influenced scholars such as Michael Fox and Marvin Pope: "With regard to the Song of Songs she is certainly correct in recognizing the equal and even dominant role of the female and the absence of male chauvinism or patriarchalism" (Pope, *The Song of Songs*, p. 210).

12. For a provocative analysis of the relationship of the Song to the story of Creation and the Fall from Eden, again see Trible, *God and the Rhetoric of Sexuality*, pp. 72–165.

❧ CHAPTER 5: *Contexts, Themes, and Motifs*

1. Carol Meyers, in "Gender Imagery in the Song of Songs," pp. 218–19, notes: "The appearance of 'mother's house' [in 3:4 and 8:2; translated as 'my mother's home' in poems 13 and 25] is striking in view of the overriding importance of 'father's house' [elsewhere]

Endnotes in the Bible. . . . The normal masculine-oriented terminology for family and/or household derives from lineage concerns, from descent and property transmission reckoned along patrilineal lines. But here in the Song we encounter a situation devoid of such concerns."

2. Wendell Berry, "A Secular Pilgrimage," *Hudson Review* 23 (1970): 401.

3. Because the imagery of artifice in the *wasfs* is so vivid, it is perhaps not surprising that scholars have speculated about its parallels to visual forms in ancient art. For example, Gillis Gerleman, "Die Bildsprache des Hohenliedes und die altägyptische Kunst," *Annual of the Swedish Theological Institute* 1 (1962): 24–30, has proposed that many of the images in the *wasfs* are based on figures from ancient Egyptian sculpture and bas-relief. Although there may be some valid parallels here, Gerleman's theory is far too limiting. By viewing the *wasfs* as literal descriptions of statues rather than as metaphorical portrayals of the human body, he misses the relationship between nature and artifice that lies at the core of this poetry.

4. See Meyers, "Gender Imagery in the Song of Songs," pp. 212–21, for further analysis of military imagery.

❧ CHAPTER 6: *Notes to the Poems*

1. See, for example, Theophile J. Meek, "The Song of Songs: Introduction and Exegesis," in *The Interpreter's Bible,* ed. George A. Buttrick (New York: Abington Press, 1956), 5:103; and Gordis, *The Song of Songs,* p. 78.

2. For another powerful association of a name with the sense of smell—here unpleasant rather than desirable—consider these lines from Middle Kingdom Egyptian verse (ca. 2000–1630 B.C.E.):

Behold, my name is detested,
Behold, more than the smell of vultures
On a summer's day when the sky is hot.

Behold, my name is detested,
Behold, [more than the smell of] a catch of fish
On a day of catching when the sky is hot.

Behold, my name is detested,
Behold, more than the smell of ducks,
More than a covert of reeds full of waterfowl.

Behold, my name is detested,
Behold, more than the smell of fishermen,
More than the creeks of the marshes where they have fished.

Behold, my name is detested,
Behold, more than the smell of crocodiles,
More than sitting by [sandbanks] full of crocodiles.

From "The Man Who Was Tired of Life," trans. R. O. Faulkner, in *The Literature of Ancient Egypt: An Anthology of Stories, Instructions, and Poetry*, ed. William Kelly Simpson (New Haven: Yale University Press, 1973), p. 205. The brackets in line 5 indicate erroneous omission; the brackets in line 15 mean the word is uncertain.

3. Meek, "The Song of Songs," p. 107. Further references to Meek in this chapter are from this work.

4. From "The Biography of Amen-em-heb," trans. John A. Wilson, in *Ancient Near Eastern Texts Relating to the Old Testament*, ed. James B. Pritchard, 3d ed. (Princeton: Princeton University Press, 1969), p. 241.

5. After arriving at this interpretation, I was pleased to find support for it in Marvin H. Pope, "A Mare in Pharaoh's Chariotry," *Bulletin of the American Schools of Oriental Research*, no. 200 (December 1970): 56–61. Pope states (pp. 59 and 61): "Pharaoh's chariots, like other chariotry in antiquity, were not drawn by a mare or mares but by stallions hitched in pairs. . . . The point of the comparison of the Lady Love with a mare in Pharaoh's chariotry in the Song of Songs 1:9 is that she is the ultimate in sex appeal." Pope provides extensive documentation for this argument, which he reiterates in *The Song of Songs*, pp. 336–41. It is interesting, too, that Rabbinic commentators in the *Midrash Rabbah* and *The Sayings of the Fathers According to Rabbi Nathan* may have read these lines similarly.

6. These remarks are from personal conversation and correspondence, August–September 1972. Rabin writes: "As for *ʿenayikh yonim = ʿenayikh kᵉyonim = ʿenayikh kᵉene yonim*, both omission of the *k-* and omission of the *nismakh* (head word of genitive relation) are perhaps not common features of biblical Hebrew, but quite well attested. . . . For instances of comparison without *k-*, see Zephaniah 3:3, Jeremiah 4:26, Job 8:9. For omission of *nismakh*, see Ezra 10:13, Psalms 19:10, Jeremiah 10:10, etc."

7. James Moffatt, trans., *A New Translation of the Bible*, rev. ed. (New York: Harper, 1935), p. 743.

8. These and other identifications of flora and fauna by Hareuveni, director of Neot Kedumim, are from personal conversation with him and correspondence with his assistant, Helen Frenkley, May–July 1972.

9. Contrary to the opinions of some Bible scholars, the quince is neither inedible nor without fragrance. Fully ripened, it has a del-

Endnotes   icate aroma; once cooked, its texture is soft and its taste quite delicious.

10. See Pritchard, *Ancient Near Eastern Texts*, p. 230.

11. This and other proposed emendations for *'al hare bater* are listed in Rudolph Kittel, ed., *Biblia Hebraica*, 7th ed. (Stuttgart: Württembergische Bibelanstalt, 1951) p. 1203; and in Gordis, *The Song of Songs*, p. 83.

12. Samuel Noah Kramer, *The Sacred Marriage Rite: Aspects of Faith, Myth, and Ritual in Ancient Sumer* (Bloomington: Indiana University Press, 1969), p. 90.

13. Gordis, *The Song of Songs*, p. 84. Further references to Gordis in this chapter are to this book.

14. See, for example, "The Love Songs and the Song of the Harper," trans. William Kelly Simpson, in Simpson, *The Literature of Ancient Egypt*, pp. 296–325. From New Kingdom love poems spoken by a woman (pp. 302–03): "My brother, my loved one, / my heart chases after your love" and "Now must I depart from the brother, / and [as I long] for your love, / my heart stands still inside me." From a New Kingdom love poem spoken by a man (p. 310): "The love of my sister lies on yonder side."

15. Edwin M. Good offers an insightful analysis of the garden as an extended metaphor in this poem in "Ezekiel's Ship: Some Extended Metaphors in the Old Testament," *Semitics* 1 (1970): 93–97.

16. Trible, *God and the Rhetoric of Sexuality*, p. 45.

17. Noting that "this verse is completely incomprehensible as it stands," Gordis also cites in his commentary (pp. 92–93) the proposed emendations of several other scholars.

18. As a poet, I find some consolation in the Japanese principle that every work of art must have one deliberate flaw or omission.

19. H. H. Rowley summarizes the many different interpretations of this word in "The Meaning of 'The Shulammite,'" *American Journal of Semitic Languages and Literatures* 56 (1930): 84–91.

20. See Kittel, *Biblia Hebraica*, p. 1210.

21. Gershom Scholem, ed., *Zohar: The Book of Splendor* (New York: Schocken Books, 1963), p. 70.

22. H. G. May, "Some Cosmic Connotations of *Mayim Rabbim*, 'Many Waters,'" *Journal of Biblical Literature* 74 (1955): 9–21.

23. Compare this poem with sixteenth- and seventeenth-century English love lyrics, both secular and religious, that use the conceit of warfare and truce as a central motif. For example, see Sir Thomas Wyatt's "I find no peace" or John Donne's "Batter my heart."

Bibliography

A comprehensive list of the writings that have influenced my work as a translator and critic would have been too cumbersome to present here. This bibliography includes all cited works, as well as other selected works specifically relevant to literary study and translation of the Song of Songs.

Albright, W. F. "Archaic Survivals in the Text of Canticles." In *Hebrew and Semitic Studies Presented to Godfrey Rolles Driver*, edited by D. W. Thomas and W. D. McHardy, pp. 1–7. Oxford: Clarendon Press, 1963.

Alter, Robert. *The Art of Biblical Poetry*. New York: Basic Books, 1985.

Berry, Wendell. "A Secular Pilgrimage." *Hudson Review* 23 (1970): 401–24.

The Bible: The New King James Version. Nashville: Thomas Nelson, 1984.

Bird, Phyllis. "Images of Women in the Old Testament." In *Religion and Sexism*, edited by Rosemary Radford Ruether, pp. 41–88. New York: Simon & Schuster, 1974.

Bly, Robert. *Leaping Poetry: An Idea with Poems and Translations*. Boston: Beacon Press, 1975.

Bodenheimer, Friedrich Simon. *Animal and Man in Bible Lands*. Leiden: E. J. Brill, 1960.

Brenner, Athalya. "Aromatics and Perfumes in the Song of Songs." *Journal for the Study of the Old Testament* 25 (1985): 75–81.

Brown, Francis, S. R. Driver, and Charles A. Briggs. *A Hebrew and English Lexicon of the Old Testament*. 1st ed., 1907; corrected impression. Oxford: Clarendon Press, 1952.

Buber, Martin. *Hasidism and Modern Man*. Translated by Maurice Friedman. New York: Harper & Row, 1966.

————. *I and Thou*. Translated by Walter Kaufmann. New York: Scribner, 1970.

————, trans. *Die Schriftwerke*. Vol. 4 of *Die Schrift*, translated by Martin Buber and Franz Rosenzweig. Cologne: Jakob Hegner Verlag, 1962.

Buber, Martin, and Franz Rosenzweig. *Die Schrift und ihre Verdeutschung*. Berlin: Schocken Verlag, 1936.

Cohen, Gerson D. "The Song of Songs and the Jewish Religious Mentality." In *The Samuel Friedland Lectures 1960–1966*. New York: Jewish Theological Seminary of America, 1966.

Cook, Albert. *The Root of the Thing: A Study of Job and the Song of Songs*. Bloomington: Indiana University Press, 1968.

Bibliography   Culley, Robert C. *Oral Formulaic Language in the Biblical Psalms.* Toronto: University of Toronto Press, 1967.

Driver, G. R. "Hebrew Poetic Diction." In *Congress Volume, Copenhagen, 1953,* pp. 26–39; Supplements to *Vetus Testamentum,* vol. 1. Leiden: E. J. Brill, 1953.

Driver, S. R. *An Introduction to the Literature of the Old Testament.* New ed., 1913; rpt. New York: Scribner, 1950.

———. *A Treatise on the Use of the Tenses in Hebrew and Some Other Syntactical Questions.* 3d ed., 1892; rpt. Oxford: Clarendon Press, 1969.

Eissfeldt, Otto. *The Old Testament: An Introduction.* Translated by Peter R. Ackroyd. New York: Harper & Row, 1965.

Elliger, K., and W. Rudolph. *Biblia Hebraica Stuttgartensia.* Stuttgart: Deutsche Bibelgesellschaft, 1977.

Exum, J. Cheryl. "A Literary and Structural Analysis of the Song of Songs." *Zeitschrift für die alttestamentliche Wissenschaft* 85 (1973): 47–79.

Feliks, Jehuda. *Šir hašširim: Ṭevaʿ ʿalilah wᵊʾaligoriyyah.* Jerusalem: Maʿᵃriv, 1974.

Fisch, Harold. *Poetry with a Purpose: Biblical Poetics and Interpretation.* Bloomington: Indiana University Press, 1988.

The Five Megilloth and Jonah: A New Translation. Introductions by H. L. Ginsberg. Philadelphia: Jewish Publication Society of America, 1969.

Follis, Elaine R., ed. *Directions in Biblical Hebrew Poetry. Journal for the Study of the Old Testament,* supp. ser., 40. Sheffield, Eng.: JSOT Press, 1987.

Fox, Everett. *In the Beginning: An English Rendition of the Book of Genesis Based on the German Version of Martin Buber and Franz Rosenzweig.* Introduction by Nahum N. Glatzer. *Response,* no. 14 (Summer 1972): 1–159.

———. *In the Beginning: A New English Rendition of the Book of Genesis.* New York: Schocken Books, 1983.

———. *Now These Are the Names: A New English Rendition of the Book of Exodus.* New York: Schocken Books, 1986.

———. "Technical Aspects of the Translation of Genesis of Martin Buber and Franz Rosenzweig." Ph.D. diss., Brandeis University, 1974.

———. "We Mean the Voice: The Buber-Rosenzweig Bible Translation." *Response,* no. 12 (Winter 1972): 29–42.

Fox, Michael V. *The Song of Songs and the Ancient Egyptian Love Songs.* Madison: University of Wisconsin Press, 1985.

Gerleman, Gillis. "Die Bildsprache des Hohenliedes und die altägyptische Kunst." *Annual of the Swedish Theological Institute* 1 (1962): 24–30.

———. *Ruth; Das Hohelied.* Biblischer Kommentar Altes Testament, vol. 18. Neukirchen-Vluyn: Neukirchener Verlag des Erziehungsvereins, 1965.

Gevirtz, Stanley. *Patterns in the Early Poetry of Israel.* Oriental Institute of Chicago Studies in Ancient Oriental Civilization, no. 32. Chicago: University of Chicago Press, 1963.

Goitein, Shelomo Dov. "Našim kᵉyoṣrot suge sifrut bammiqra'." In *'Iyyunim* *Bibliography*
bammiqra'*, pp. 248–317. Tel Aviv: Yavneh, 1967.

———. "Šir hašširim." In *'Omanut hassippur bammiqra'*, pp. 104–10. Jerusalem: Jewish Agency Aliyah and Youth Division, 1957.

Good, Edwin M. "Ezekiel's Ship: Some Extended Metaphors in the Old Testament." *Semitics* 1 (1970): 79–103.

Good News Bible: The Bible in Today's English Version. New York: American Bible Society, 1976.

Gordis, Robert. *The Song of Songs: A Study, Modern Translation, and Commentary.* New York: Jewish Theological Seminary of America, 1961.

Goulder, Michael D. *The Song of Fourteen Songs. Journal for the Study of the Old Testament*, supp. ser., 36. Sheffield, Eng.: JSOT Press, 1986.

Gray, George Buchanan. *The Forms of Hebrew Poetry: Considered with Special Reference to the Criticism and Interpretation of the Old Testament.* 1st ed., 1915; rpt., with Prolegomenon by David Noel Freedman. New York: Ktav, 1972.

Greenstein, Edward L. "Theories of Modern Bible Translation." *Prooftexts* 3 (1983): 9–39.

The Holy Bible: Containing the Old and New Testaments (Authorized or King James Version). Translated out of the Original Tongues and with the Former Translations Diligently Compared & Revised. Set Forth in 1611 and Commonly Known as the King James Version. New York: American Bible Society, n.d.

The Holy Bible: New International Version, Containing the Old Testament and the New Testament. Grand Rapids: Zondervan Bible Publishers, 1978.

The Holy Bible: New Revised Standard Version with Apocrypha. Oxford: Oxford University Press, 1989.

The Holy Bible: Revised Standard Version, Containing the Old and New Testaments. Translated from the Original Tongues, Being the Version Set Forth A.D. 1611, Revised A.D. 1881–1885 and A.D. 1901, Compared with the Most Ancient Authorities and Revised A.D. 1952. New York: Thomas Nelson, 1946–52.

The Holy Scriptures According to the Masoretic Text: A New Translation. With the Aid of Previous Versions and with Constant Consultation of Jewish Authorities. Philadelphia: Jewish Publication Society of America, 1917.

Jacobsen, Thorkild, and John A. Wilson, trans. *Most Ancient Verse.* Introduction by David Grene. Chicago: Oriental Institute of the University of Chicago, 1963.

The Jerusalem Bible. Edited by Alexander Jones. Garden City, N.Y.: Doubleday, 1966.

Kittel, Rudolph, ed. *Biblia Hebraica.* 7th ed. Stuttgart: Württembergische Bibelanstalt, 1951.

Koehler, Ludwig, and Walter Baumgartner. *Lexicon in Veteris Testamenti Libros.* 2d ed. Leiden: E. J. Brill, 1958.

Bibliography   Kosmala, Hans. "Form and Structure in Ancient Hebrew Poetry (A New Approach)." *Vetus Testamentum* 14 (1964): 423–45; 16 (1966): 152–80.

Kramer, Samuel Noah. *The Sacred Marriage Rite: Aspects of Faith, Myth, and Ritual in Ancient Sumer.* Bloomington: Indiana University Press, 1969.

Krinetzki, Leo, O. S. B. *Das Hohe Lied: Kommentar zu Gestalt und Kerygma eines alttestamentliche Liebesliedes.* Düsseldorf: Patmos-Verlag, 1964.

Kristeva, Julia. *Tales of Love.* Translated by Leon S. Roudiez. New York: Columbia University Press, 1987.

Kugel, James L. *The Idea of Biblical Poetry: Parallelism and Its History.* New Haven: Yale University Press, 1981.

Landsberger, Franz. "Poetic Units Within the Song of Songs." *Journal of Biblical Literature* 73 (1954): 203–16.

Landy, Francis. "Beauty and the Enigma: An Inquiry into Some Interrelated Episodes of the Song of Songs." *Journal for the Study of the Old Testament* 17 (1980): 55–106.

———. *Paradoxes of Paradise: Identity and Difference in the Song of Songs.* Sheffield, Eng.: Almond Press, 1983.

———. "The Song of Songs and the Garden of Eden." *Journal of Biblical Literature* 98 (1979): 513–28.

Lord, Albert. *The Singer of Tales.* Cambridge, Mass.: Harvard University Press, 1960.

Lys, Daniel. *Le plus beau chant de la création: Commentaire du Cantique des cantiques.* Lectio Divina, 51. Paris: Editions Cerf, 1968.

Mandelkern, Solomon. *Veteris Testamenti Concordantiae Hebraicae Atque Chaldaicae.* 2 vols. 2d ed., 1937; rpt. Graz: Akademische Druck- und Verlagsanstalt, 1955.

May, H. G. "Some Cosmic Connotations of *Mayim Rabbim,* 'Many Waters.'" *Journal of Biblical Literature* 74 (1955): 9–21.

Meek, Theophile J. "The Song of Songs: Introduction and Exegesis." In *The Interpreter's Bible,* edited by George A. Buttrick, 5:91–148. New York: Abington Press, 1956.

Meyers, Carol. *Discovering Eve: Ancient Israelite Women in Context.* New York: Oxford University Press, 1988.

———. "Gender Imagery in the Song of Songs." *Hebrew Annual Review* 10 (1986): 209–23.

Moffatt, James, trans. *A New Translation of the Bible.* Rev. ed. New York: Harper, 1935.

Moldenke, Harold N., and Alma L. Moldenke. *Plants of the Bible.* New York: Ronald Press, 1952.

Muilenburg, James. "Form Criticism and Beyond." *Journal of Biblical Literature* 88 (1969): 1–18.

———. "A Study in Hebrew Rhetoric: Repetition and Style." In *Congress Volume, Copenhagen, 1953,* pp. 97–111; Supplements to *Vetus Testamentum,* vol. 1. Leiden: E. J. Brill, 1953.

Murphy, Roland E. "Towards a Commentary on the Song of Songs." *Catholic Biblical Quarterly* 39 (1977): 482–96.

———. *Wisdom Literature: Job, Proverbs, Ruth, Canticles, Ecclesiastes, and Esther.* The Forms of the Old Testament Literature, 13: 97–124. Grand Rapids, Mich.: Eerdmans, 1981.

The New American Bible. Translated from the Original Languages with Critical Use of All the Ancient Sources by Members of the Catholic Biblical Association of America. New York: P. J. Kennedy, 1970.

New American Standard Bible. Reference ed. La Habra, Calif.: Foundation Press Publications for the Lockman Foundation, 1973.

The New English Bible: The Old Testament. Oxford: Oxford University Press; Cambridge: Cambridge University Press, 1970.

The New Jerusalem Bible. Edited by Henry Wansbrough. Garden City, N.Y.: Doubleday, 1985.

Nielsen, Eduard. *Oral Tradition: A Modern Problem in Old Testament.* Foreword by H. H. Rowley. Studies in Biblical Theology, 11. Chicago: Alec R. Allenson, 1954.

O'Connor, M. *Hebrew Verse Structure.* Winona Lake, Ind.: Eisenbrauns, 1980.

Pfeiffer, Robert H. *Introduction to the Old Testament.* 2d ed. New York: Harper, 1948.

Pope, Marvin H. "A Mare in Pharaoh's Chariotry." *Bulletin of the American Schools of Oriental Research*, no. 200 (December 1970): 56–61.

———. *The Song of Songs: A New Translation with Introduction and Commentary.* New York: Doubleday, 1977.

Pound, Ezra, and Noel Stock, trans. *Love Poems of Ancient Egypt.* New York: New Directions, 1962.

Preminger, Alex, and Edward L. Greenstein, eds. *The Hebrew Bible in Literary Criticism.* New York: Ungar, 1986.

Pritchard, James B., ed. *Ancient Near Eastern Texts Relating to the Old Testament.* 3d ed. with supplement. Princeton: Princeton University Press, 1969.

Rabin, Chaim. "The Song of Songs and Tamil Poetry." *Studies in Religion* 3 (1973–74): 205–19.

Rauber, D. F. "Literary Values in the Bible: The Book of Ruth." *Journal of Biblical Literature* 89 (1970): 27–37.

The Revised English Bible. Oxford: Oxford University Press; Cambridge: Cambridge University Press, 1989.

Ringgren, Helmer. *Das Hohe Lied.* Das Alte Testament Deutsch, 16:257–93. 2d ed. Göttingen: Vanderhoeck & Ruprecht, 1967.

Robert, A., P. S. S., and R. Tournay, O. P., with A. Feuillet, P. S. S. *Le Cantique des cantiques: Traduction et commentaire.* Paris: J. Gabalda, 1963.

Robinson, Theodore H. "Hebrew Poetic Form: The English Tradition." In *Congress Volume, Copenhagen, 1953*, pp. 128–49; Supplements to *Vetus Testamentum*, vol. 1. London: E. J. Brill, 1953.

Bibliography ———. *The Poetry of the Old Testament*. London: Gerald Duckworth, 1947.

Rosenzweig, Franz. *The Star of Redemption*. Translated from the 2d ed. of 1930 by William W. Hallo; foreword by N. N. Glatzer. Boston: Beacon Press, 1972.

Rowley, H. H. "The Interpretation of the Song of Songs." In *The Servant of the Lord and Other Essays on the Old Testament*, pp. 197–245. 2d ed. Oxford: Basil Blackwell, 1965.

———. "The Meaning of 'The Shulammite.'" *American Journal of Semitic Languages and Literatures* 56 (1930): 84–91.

Rudolph, Wilhelm. *Das Buch Ruth; Das Hohe Lied; Die Klagelieder*. Kommentar zum Alten Testament, 17:1–3. Gütersloh: Gerd Mohn, 1962.

Schoff, Wilfred H., ed. *The Song of Songs: A Symposium*. Philadelphia: Commercial Museum, 1924.

Scholem, Gershom. "At the Completion of Buber's Translation of the Bible," translated by Michael A. Meyer. In *The Messianic Idea in Judaism and Other Essays on Jewish Spirituality*, pp. 314–19. New York: Schocken Books, 1971.

———, ed. *Zohar: The Book of Splendor*. New York: Schocken Books, 1963.

Segal, M. H. "The Song of Songs." *Vetus Testamentum* 12 (1962): 470–90.

Segert, Stanislav. "Problems of Hebrew Prosody." In *Congress Volume, Oxford, 1959*, pp. 283–91; Supplements to *Vetus Testamentum*, vol. 7. Leiden: E. J. Brill, 1960.

Shea, Williams H. "The Chiastic Structure of the Song of Songs." *Zeitschrift für die alttestamentliche Wissenschaft* 92 (1980): 378–96.

Simpson, William Kelly, ed. *The Literature of Ancient Egypt: An Anthology of Stories, Instructions, and Poetry*. New ed., with translations by R. O. Faulkner, Edward F. Wente, Jr., and William Kelly Simpson. New Haven: Yale University Press, 1973.

Smith, J. M. Powis, et al., trans. *The Complete Bible: An American Translation. The Old Testament*. Chicago: University of Chicago Press, 1939.

Soulen, Richard N. "The *Wasfs* of the Song of Songs and Hermeneutic." *Journal of Biblical Literature* 86 (1967): 183–90.

Spitzer, Leo. "Linguistics and Literary History." In *Linguistics and Literary History: Essays in Stylistics*, pp. 1–39. Princeton: Princeton University Press, 1948.

Tanakh: The Holy Scriptures. The New JPS Translation According to the Traditional Hebrew Text. Philadelphia: The Jewish Publication Society of America, 1985.

Trible, Phyllis. "Depatriarchalizing in Biblical Interpretation." *Journal of American Academy of Religion* 41 (1973): 30–48.

———. *God and the Rhetoric of Sexuality*. Philadelphia: Fortress Press, 1978.

Wakeman, Mary, ed. "Images of Women in the Bible." (Contributors: Mary Callaway, Cheryl Exum, Marianne Micks, Mary Wakeman, and Martha Wilson.) *Women's Caucus–Religious Studies Newsletter* 2, no. 3 (Fall 1974): 1, 3–6, 10.

Waskow, Arthur. "The Bible's Sleeping Beauty and Her Great-Grand-daughters." *Tikkun* 4, no. 2 (March/April 1989): 39–41, 125–28.

Waterman, Leroy. *The Song of Songs: Translated and Interpreted as a Dramatic Poem*. Ann Arbor: University of Michigan Press, 1948.

Webster, Edwin C. "Pattern in the Song of Songs." *Journal for the Study of the Old Testament* 22 (1982): 73–93.

Wetzstein, J. G. von. "Die syrische Dreschtafel." *Zeitschrift für Ethnologie* 5 (1873): 270–302.

Whallon, William. "Formulaic Poetry in the Old Testament." *Comparative Literature* 15 (1963): 1–14.

White, John B. *A Study of the Language of Love in the Song of Songs and Ancient Egyptian Poetry*. Society of Biblical Literature Dissertation Series, 38. Missoula, Mont.: Scholars Press, 1978.

Yoder, Perry. "A-B Pairs and Oral Composition in Hebrew Poetry." *Vetus Testamentum* 21 (1971): 470–89.

———. "Biblical Hebrew." In *Versification: Major Language Types*, edited by W. K. Wimsatt, pp. 52–65. New York: New York University Press, 1972.

Zohary, Michael, and Naomi Feinbrun. *Flora Palaestina*. 2 vols. Jerusalem: Israel Academy of Sciences and Humanities, 1966.

The Songs of Songs: A New Translation and Interpretation was set in Galliard by Wilsted & Taylor, Oakland, California. Galliard was designed by Matthew Carter in 1978 for the Mergenthaler Company and was based on the sixteenth-century typefaces of the French type designer Robert Granjon.

The Hebrew text was set in Hadassah by Simcha Graphics, Brooklyn, New York. Hadassah was created by Henri Fried-lander, who is considered the master of Hebrew calligraphy today. Begun in Germany in the early 1930s, the design for Hadassah was interrupted by World War II and completed in the early 1950s in Israel. One of the first modern Hebrew text faces, it combines twentieth-century principles of design with elements of ancient calligraphic styles.